EASY COLO
BOOK FOR
LOVERS OF OLD
CLASSIC BOLD
CARS
FOR ADULTS

THIS BOOK BELONGS TO

DADDY - FLASH
....

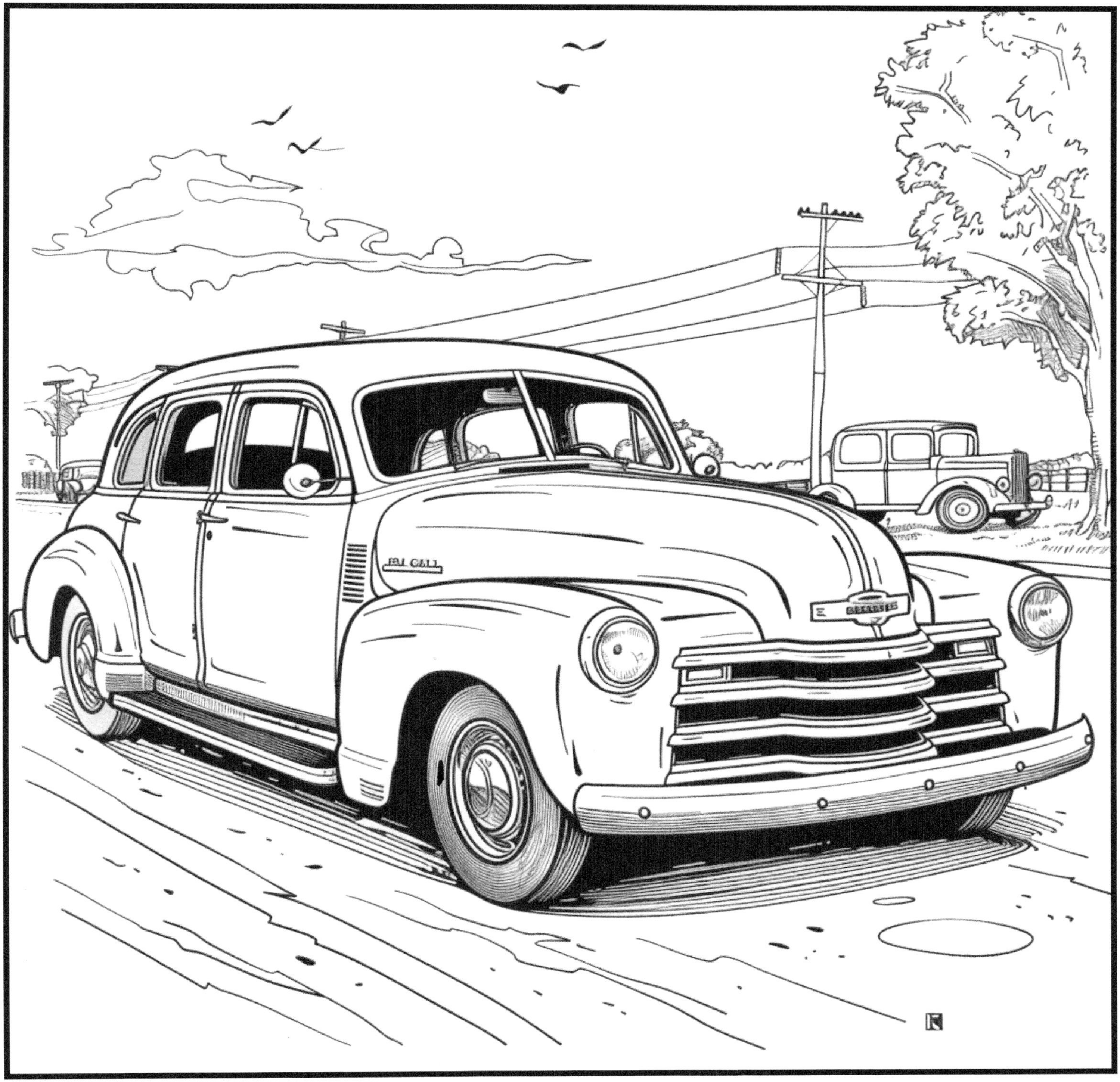

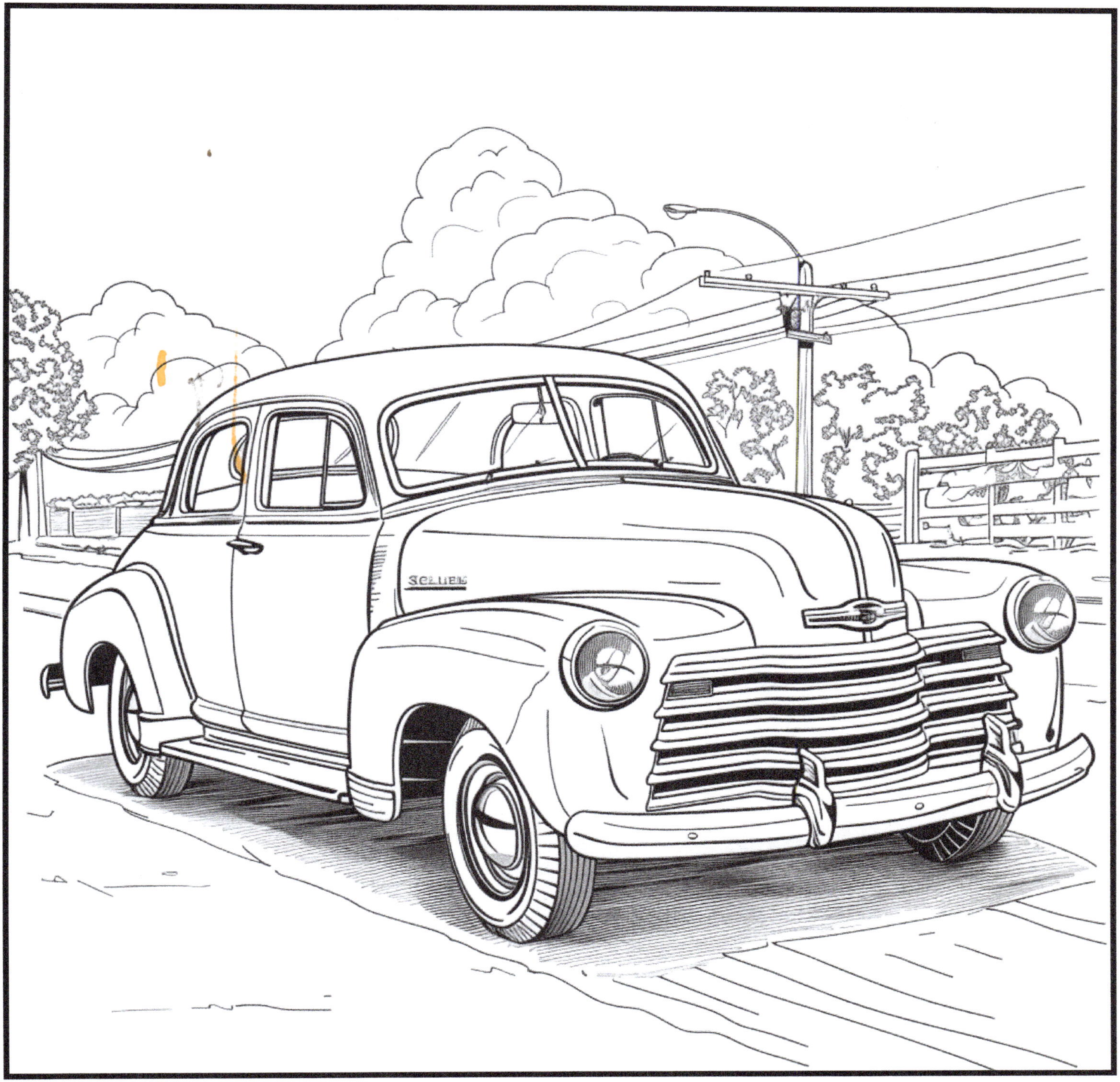

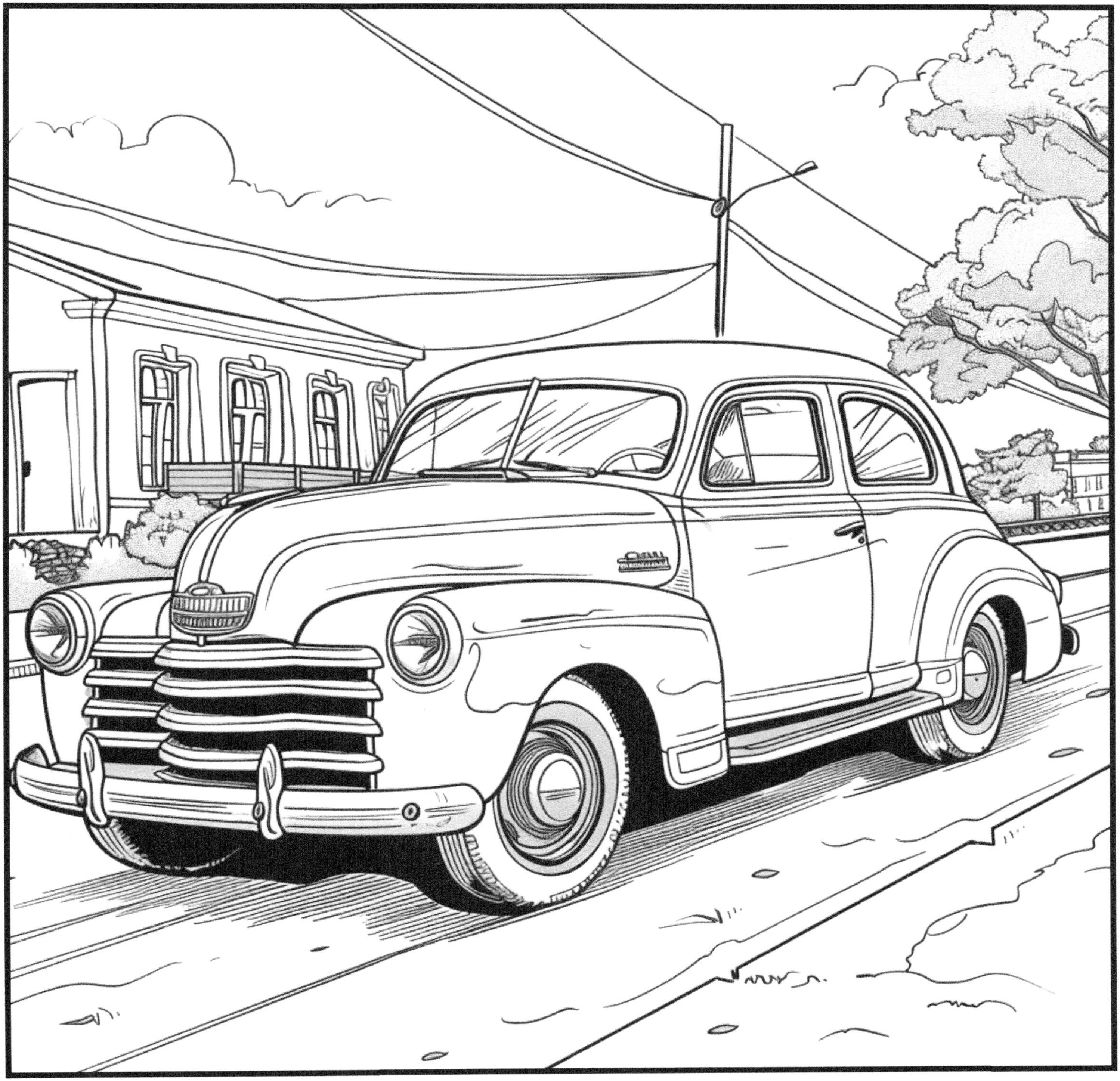

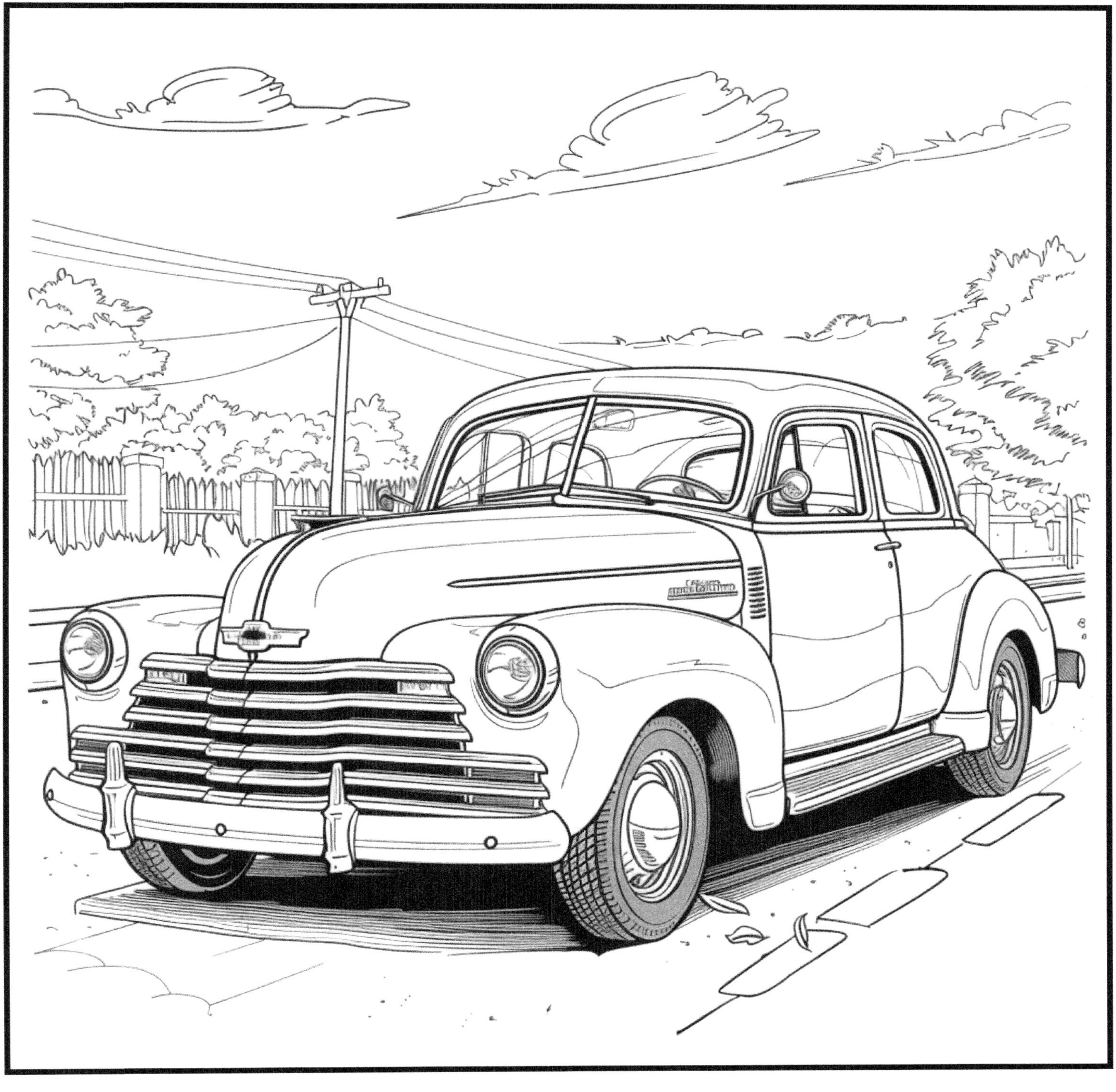

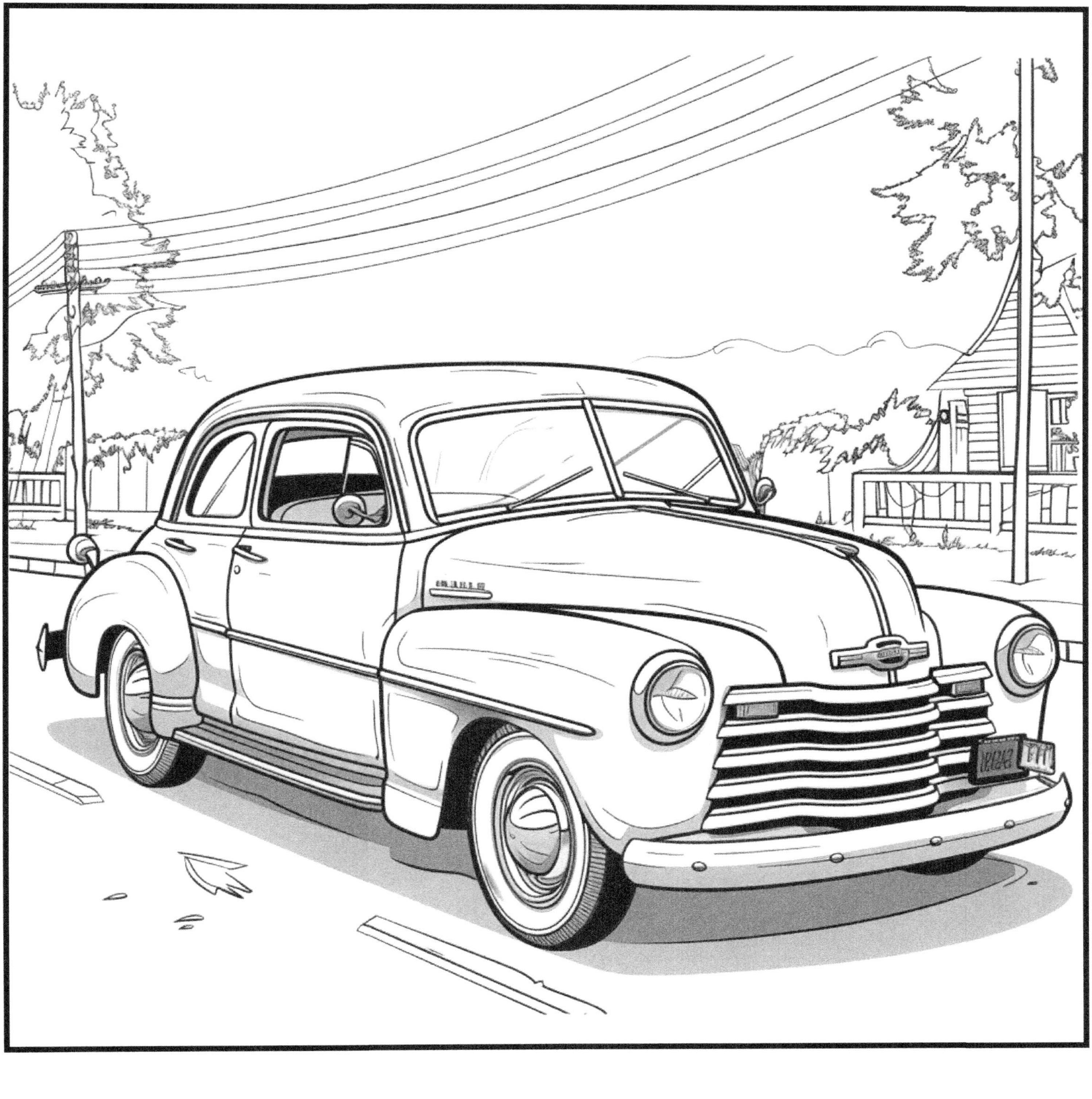

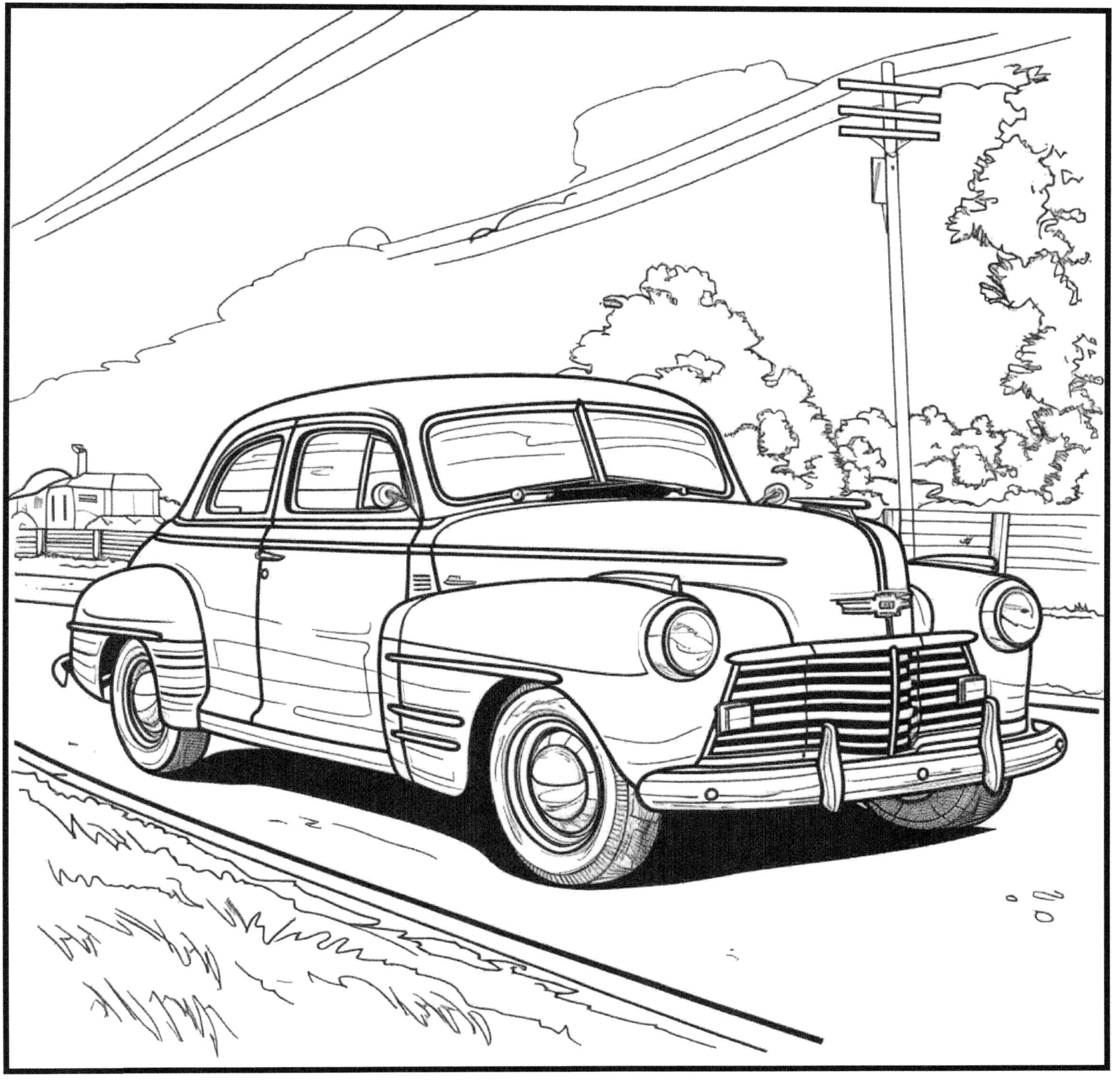

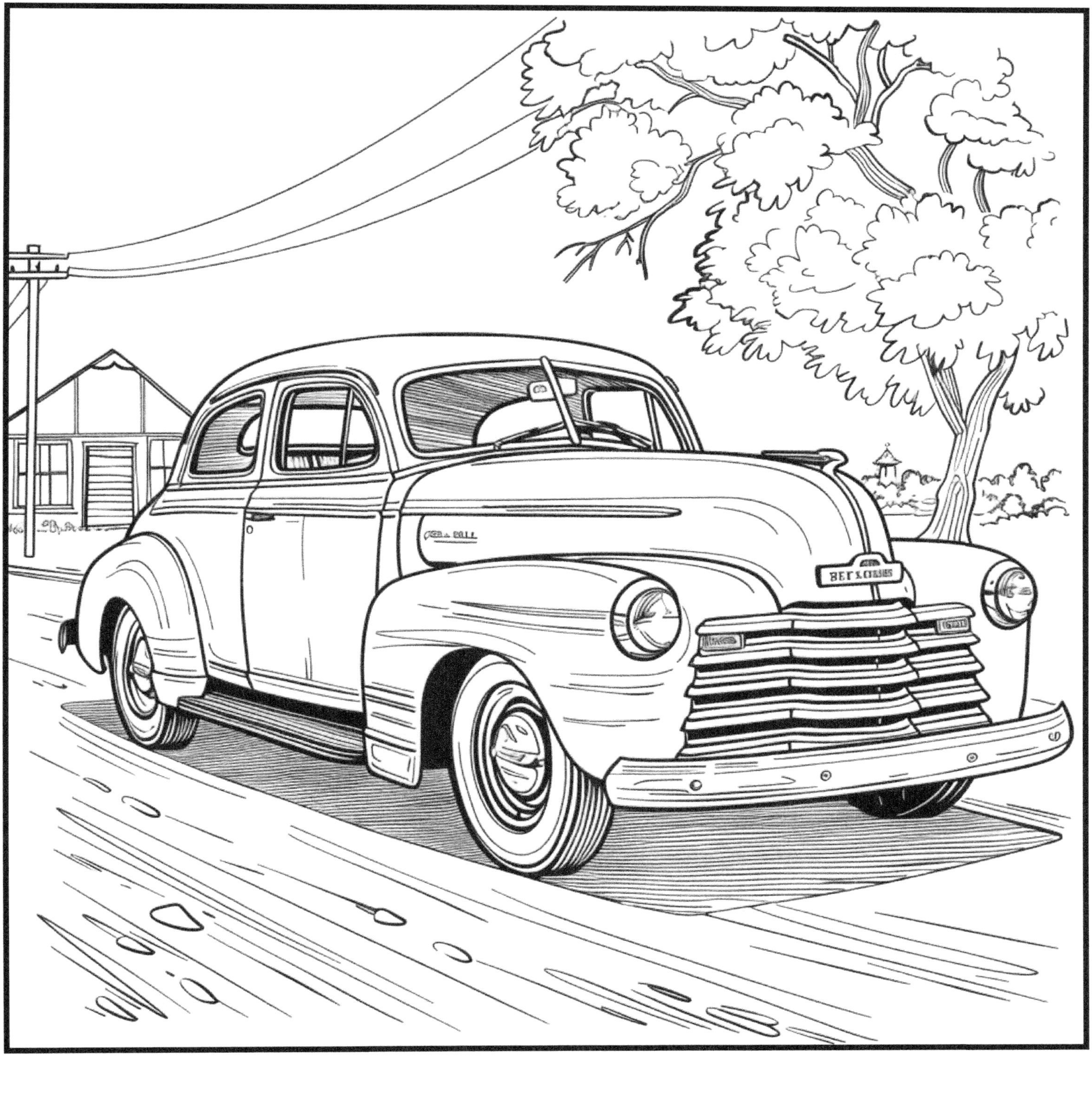

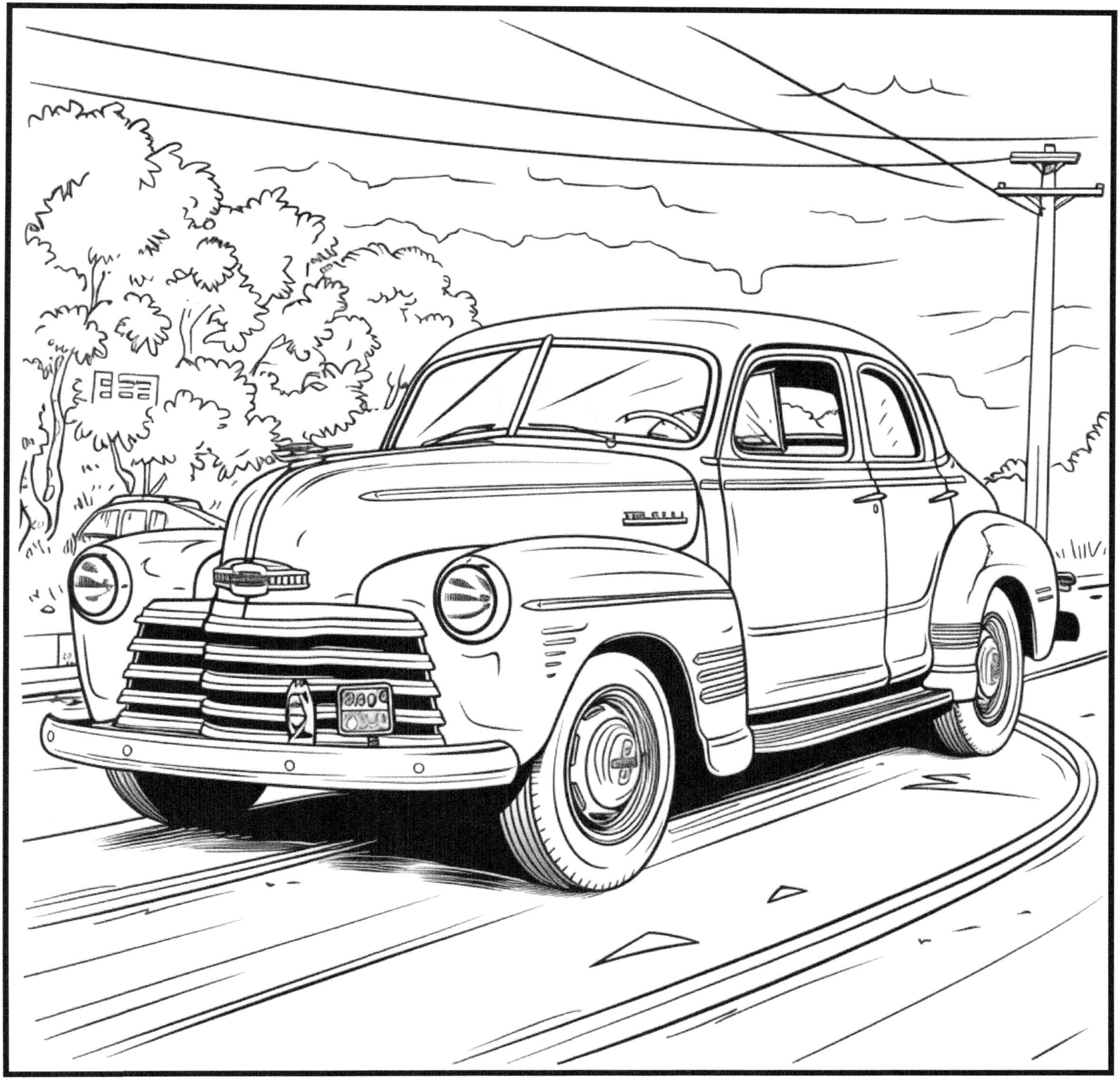

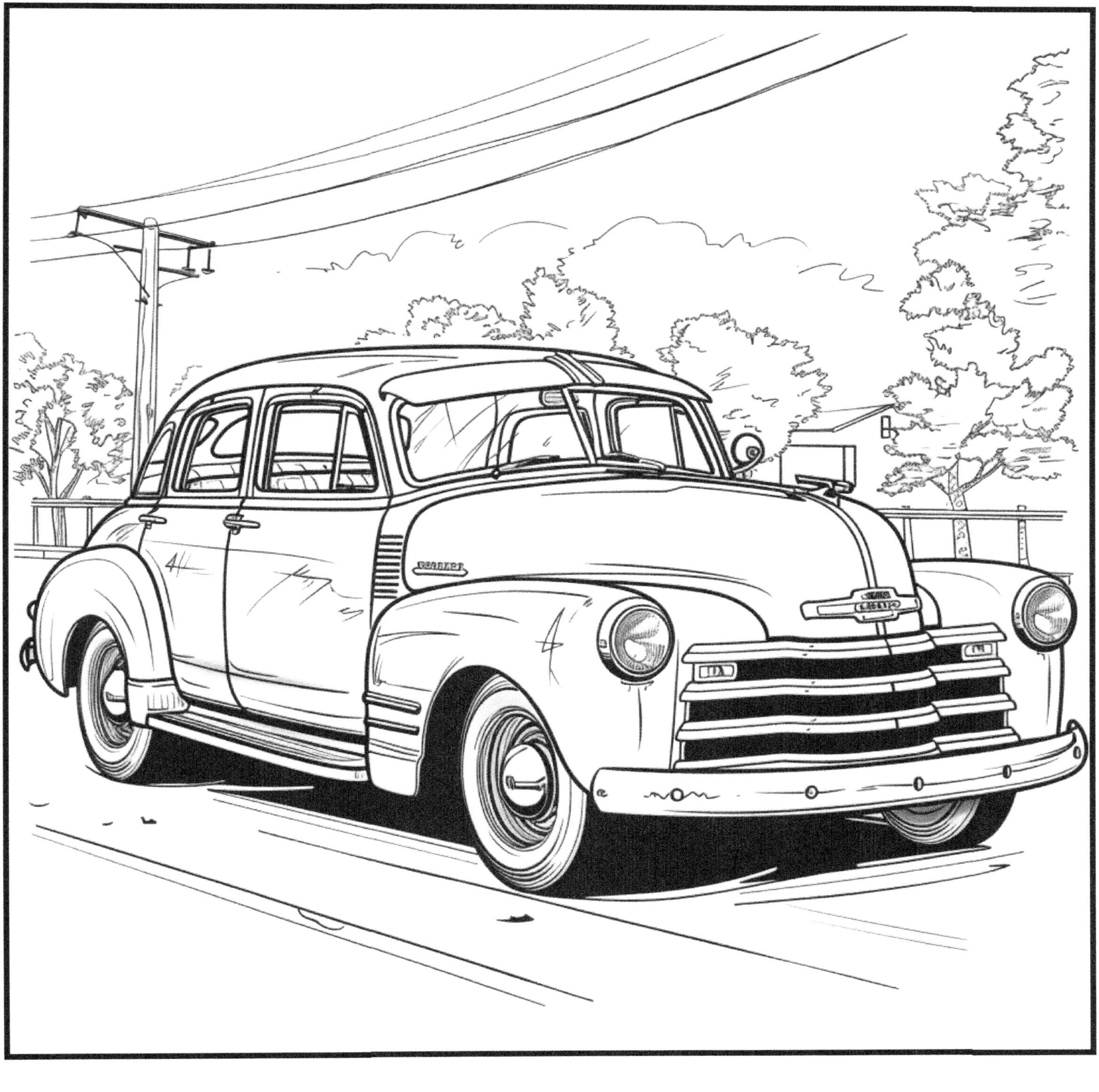

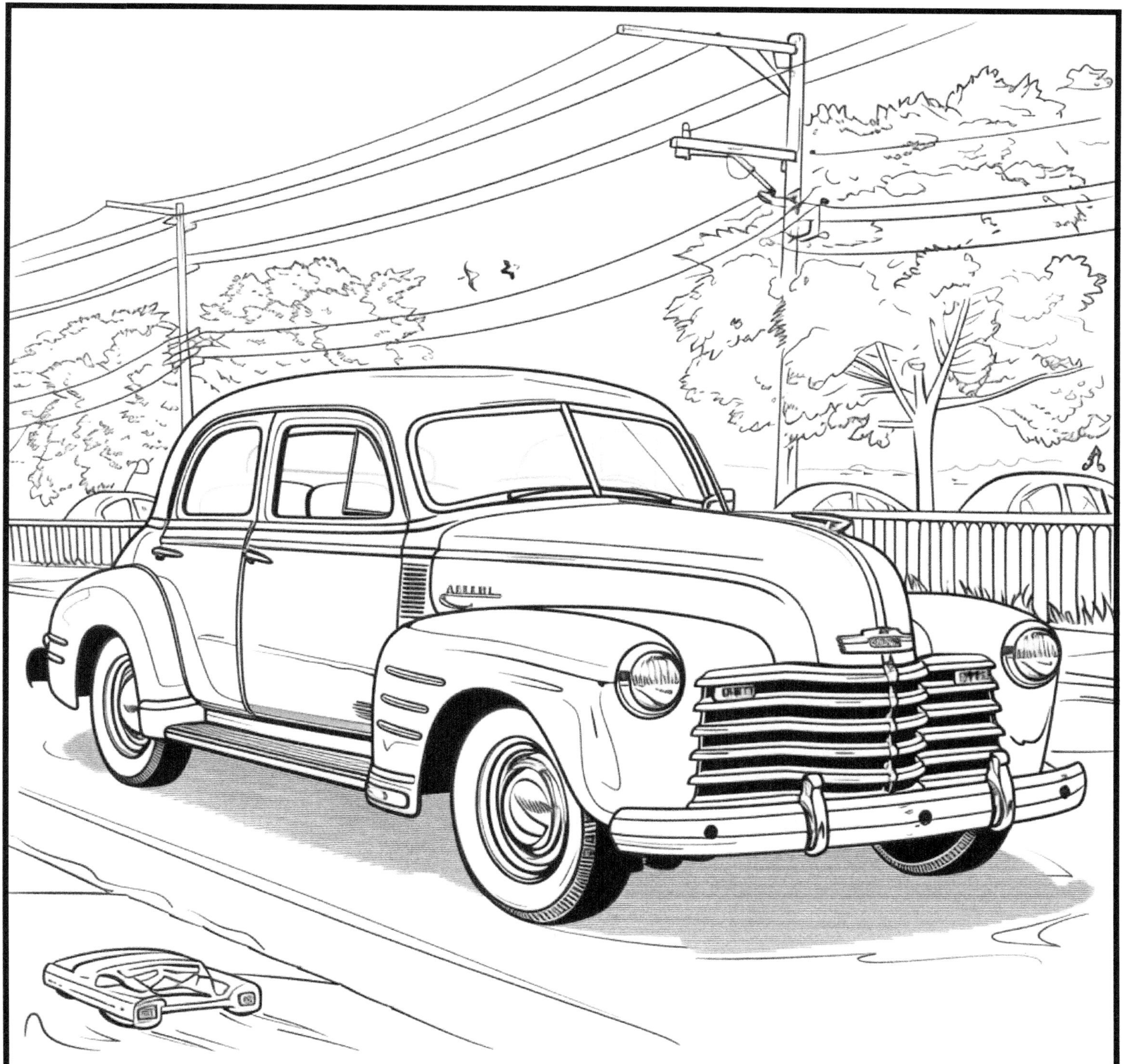

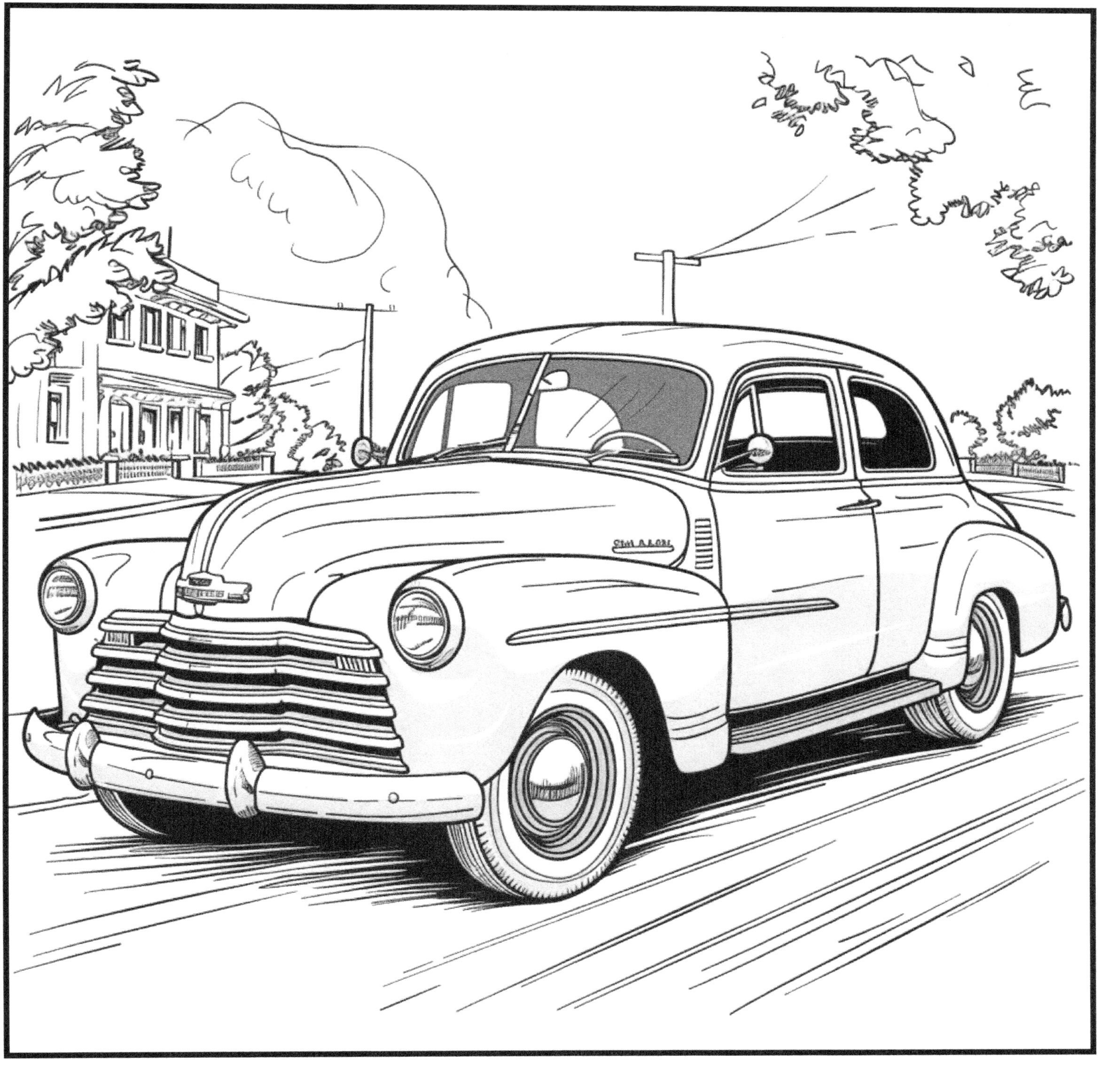

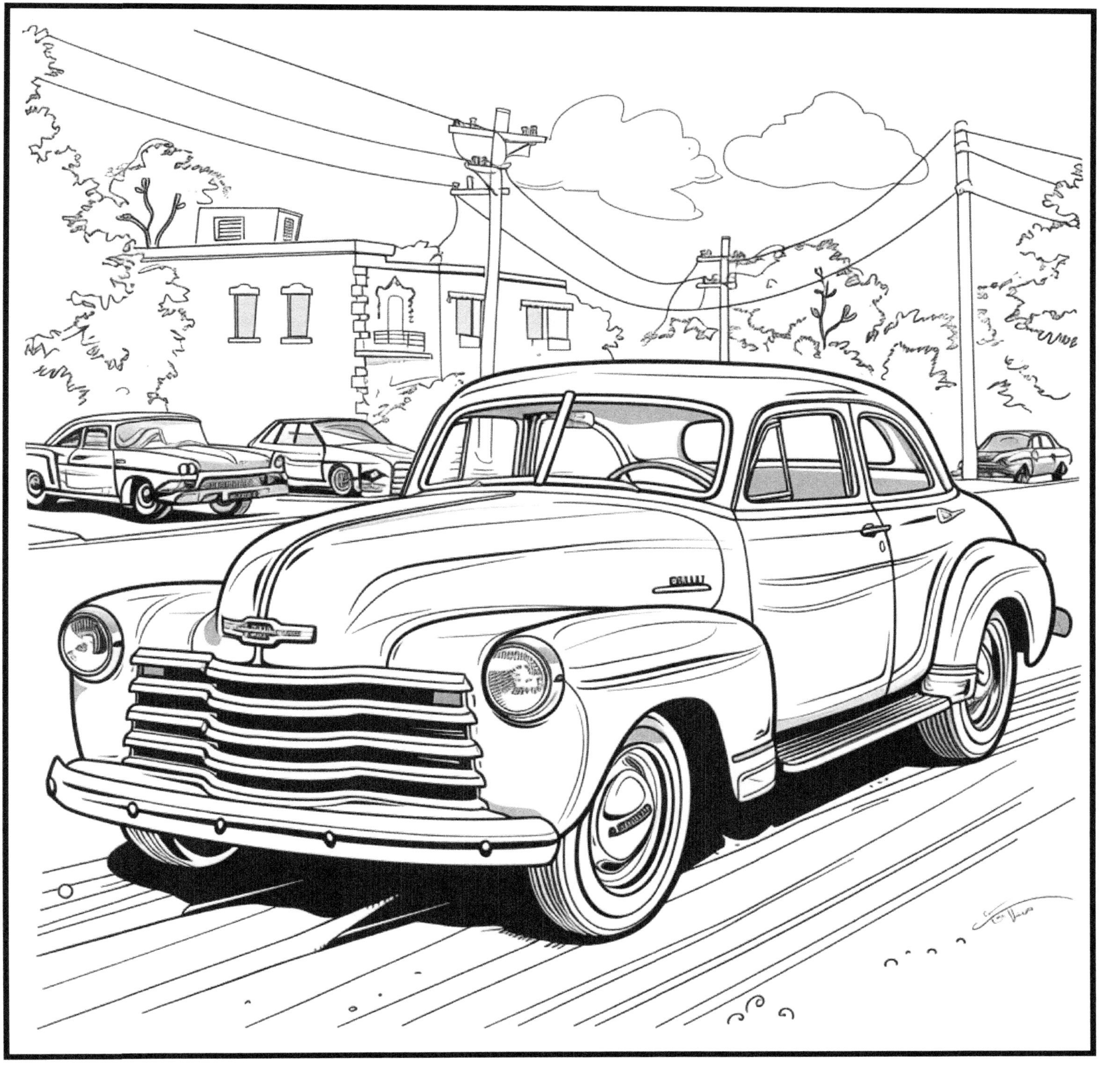

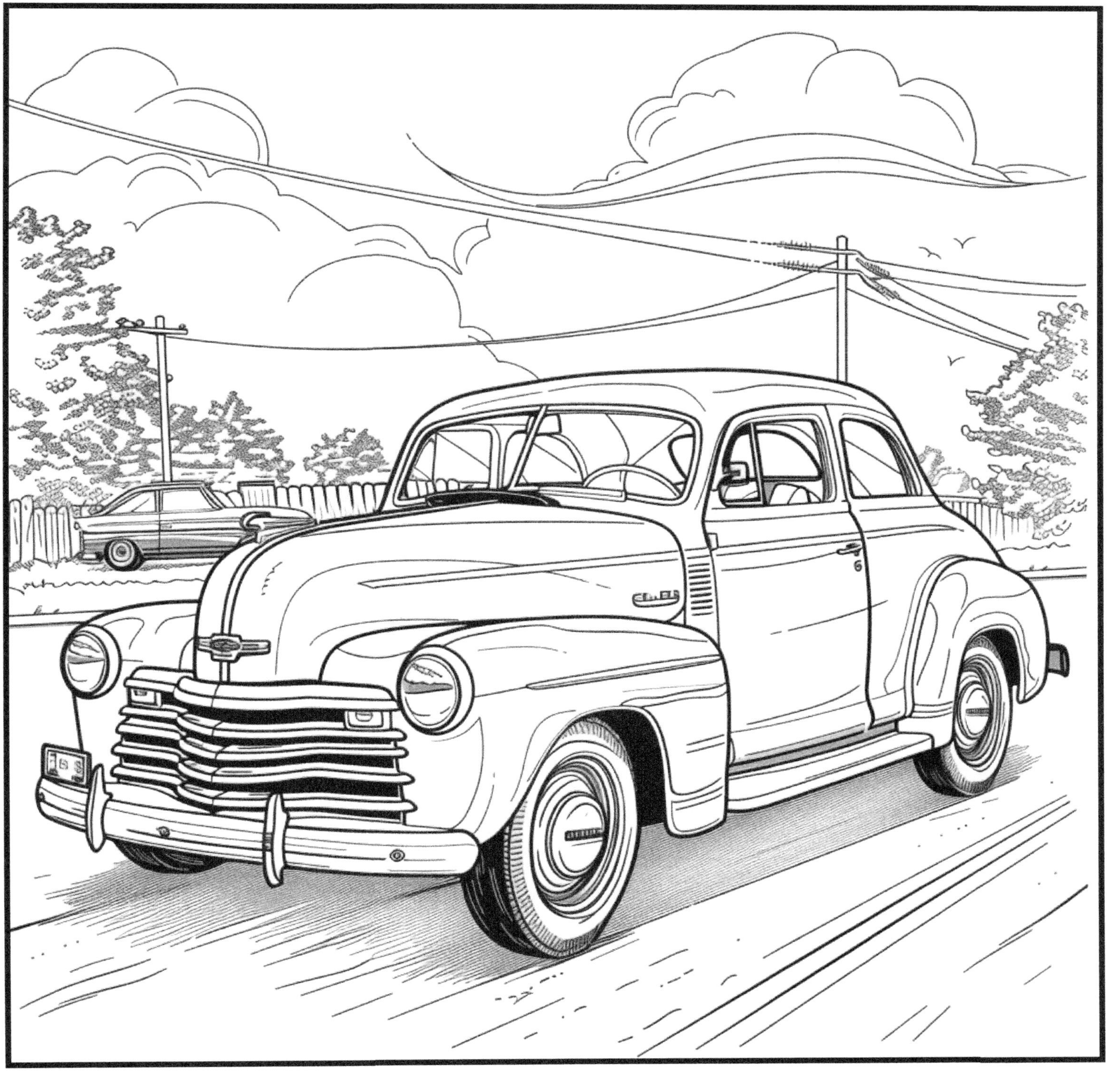

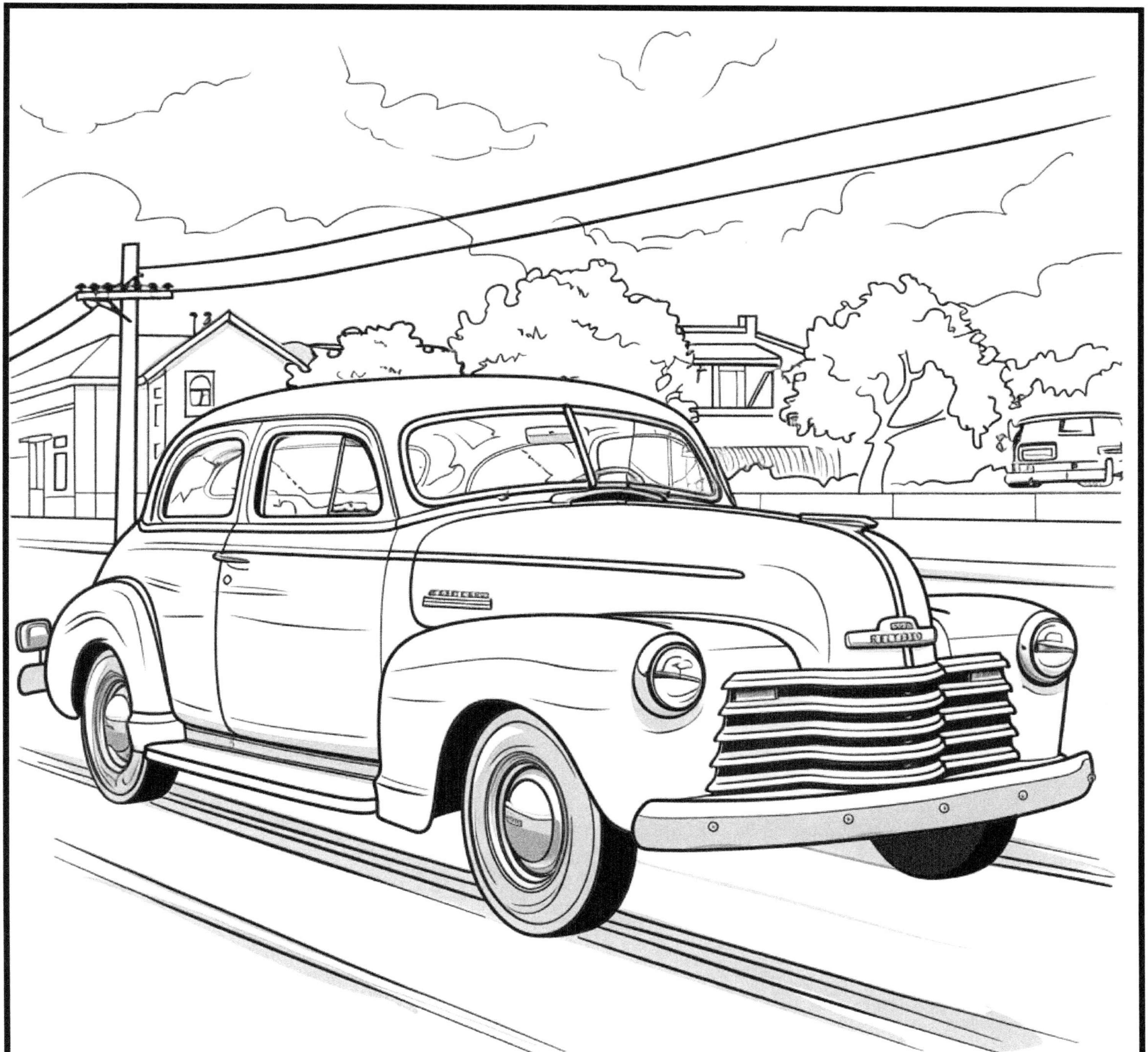

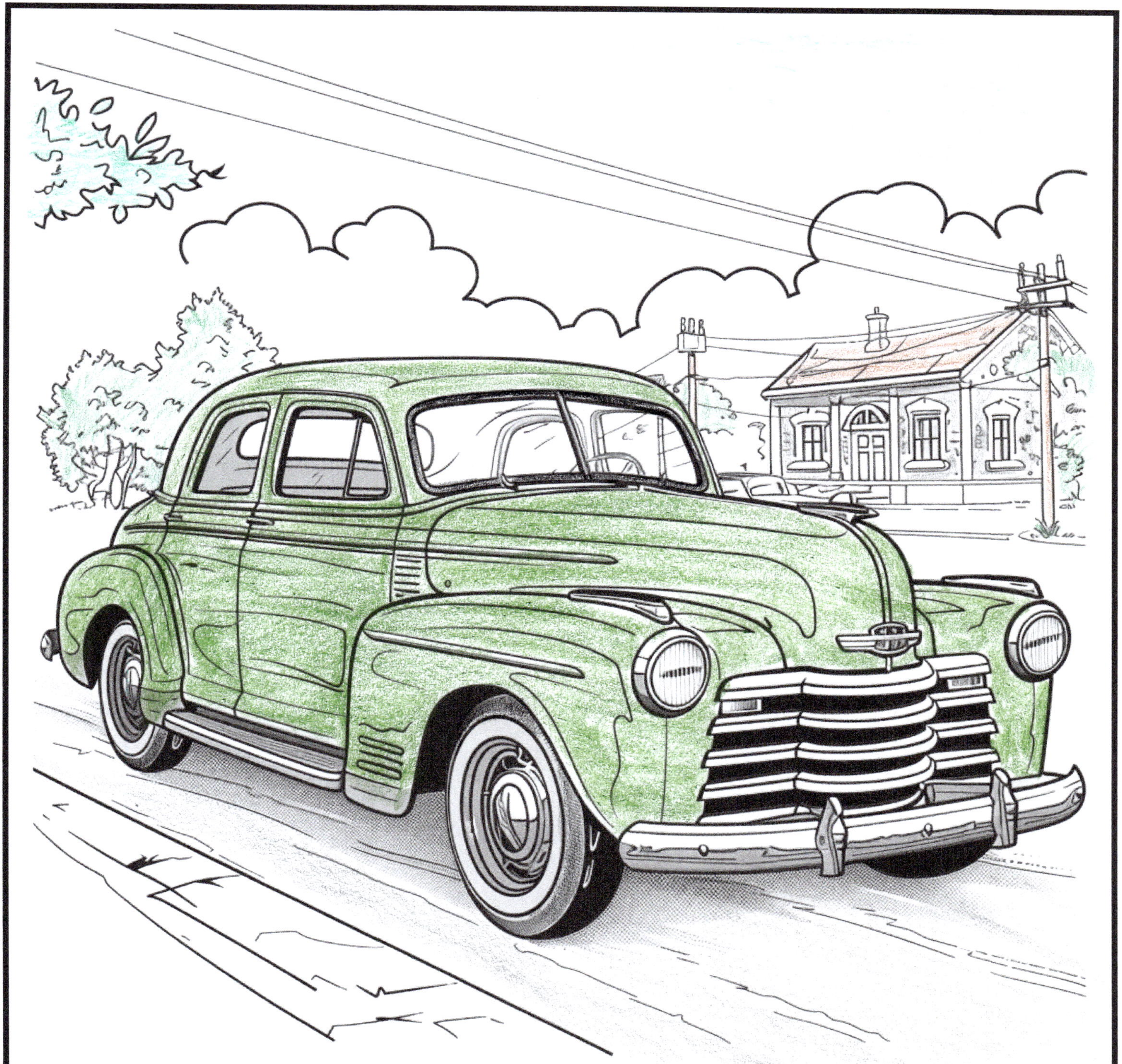

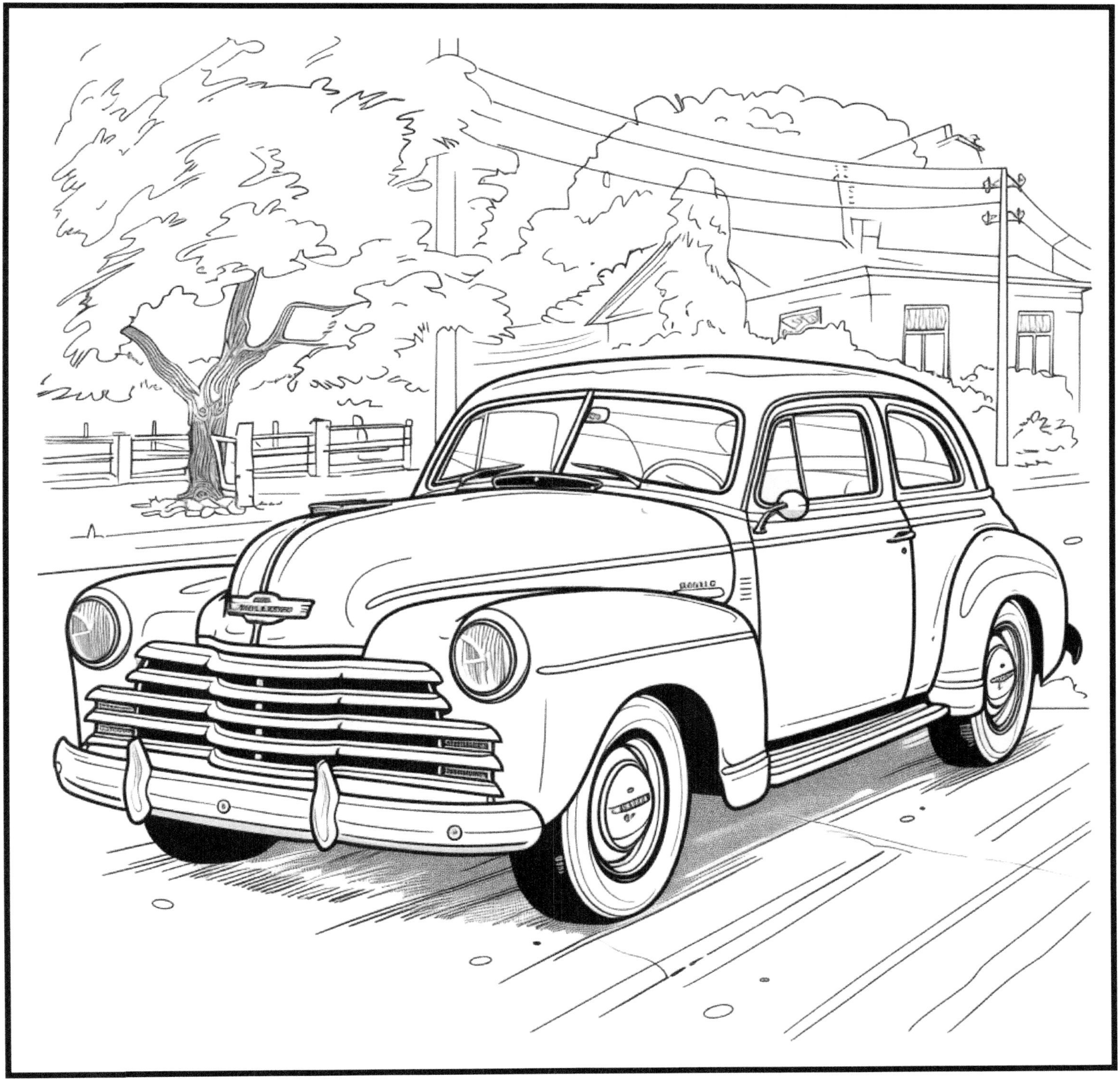

31 - 12 - 24

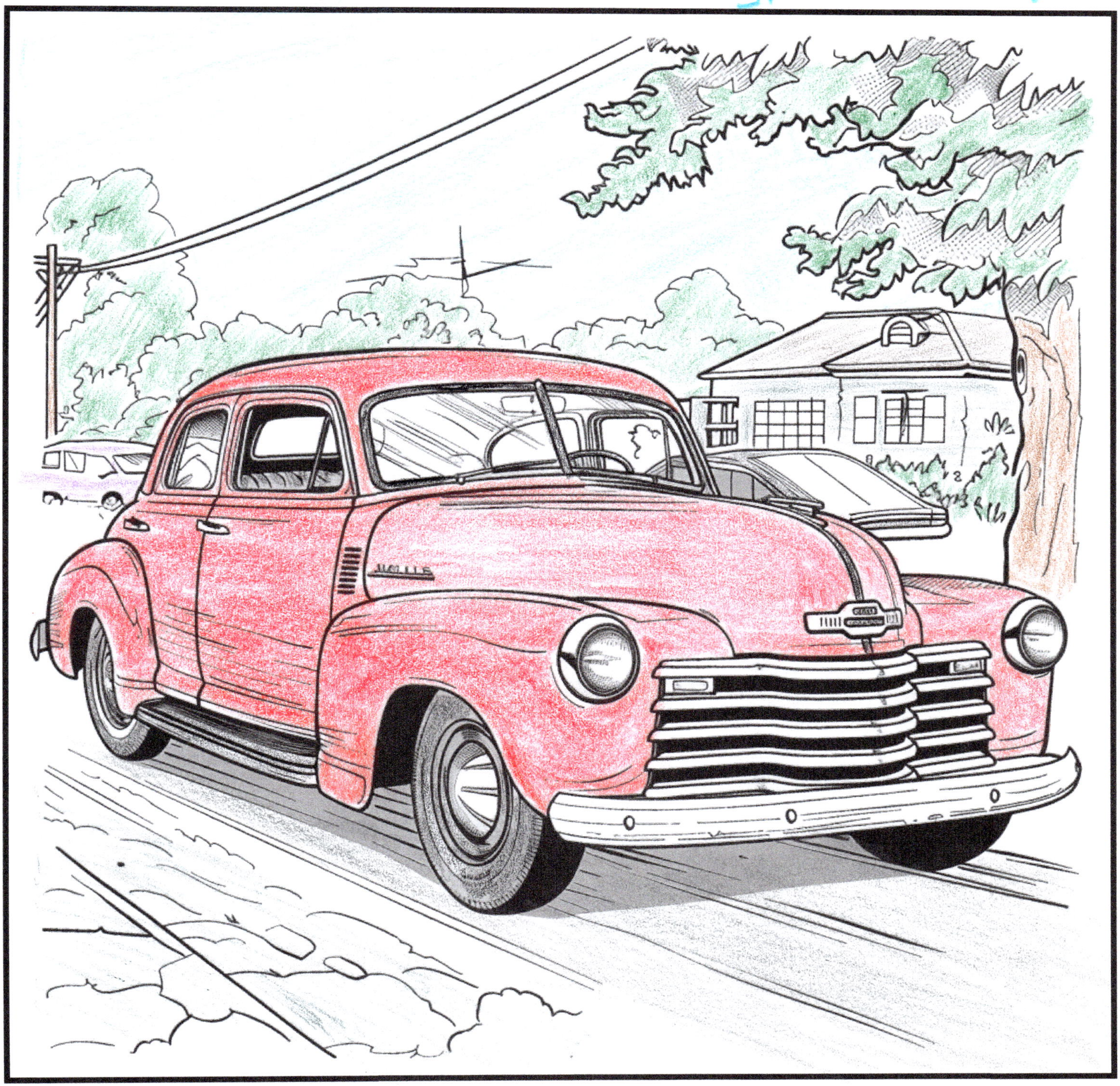

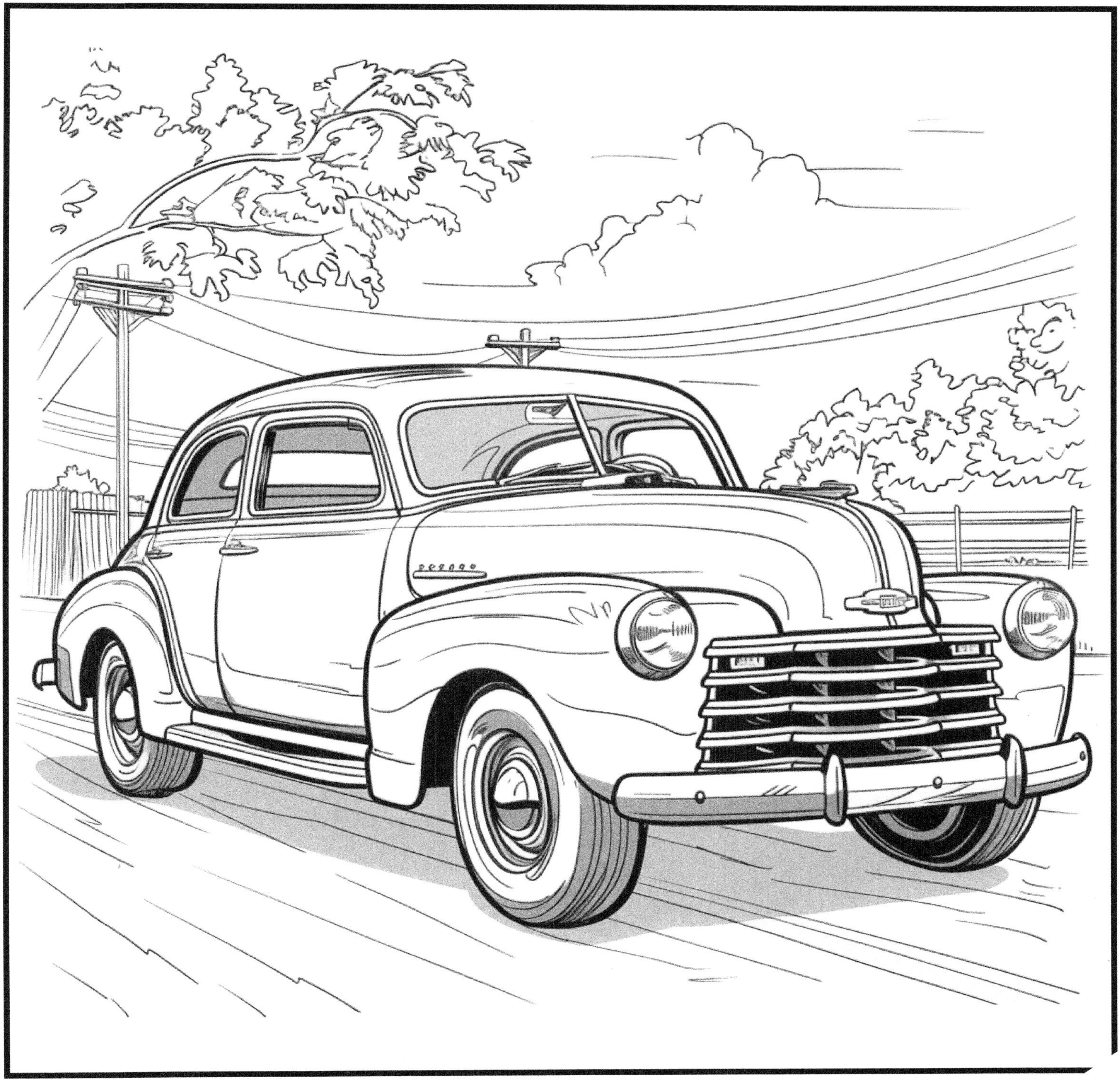

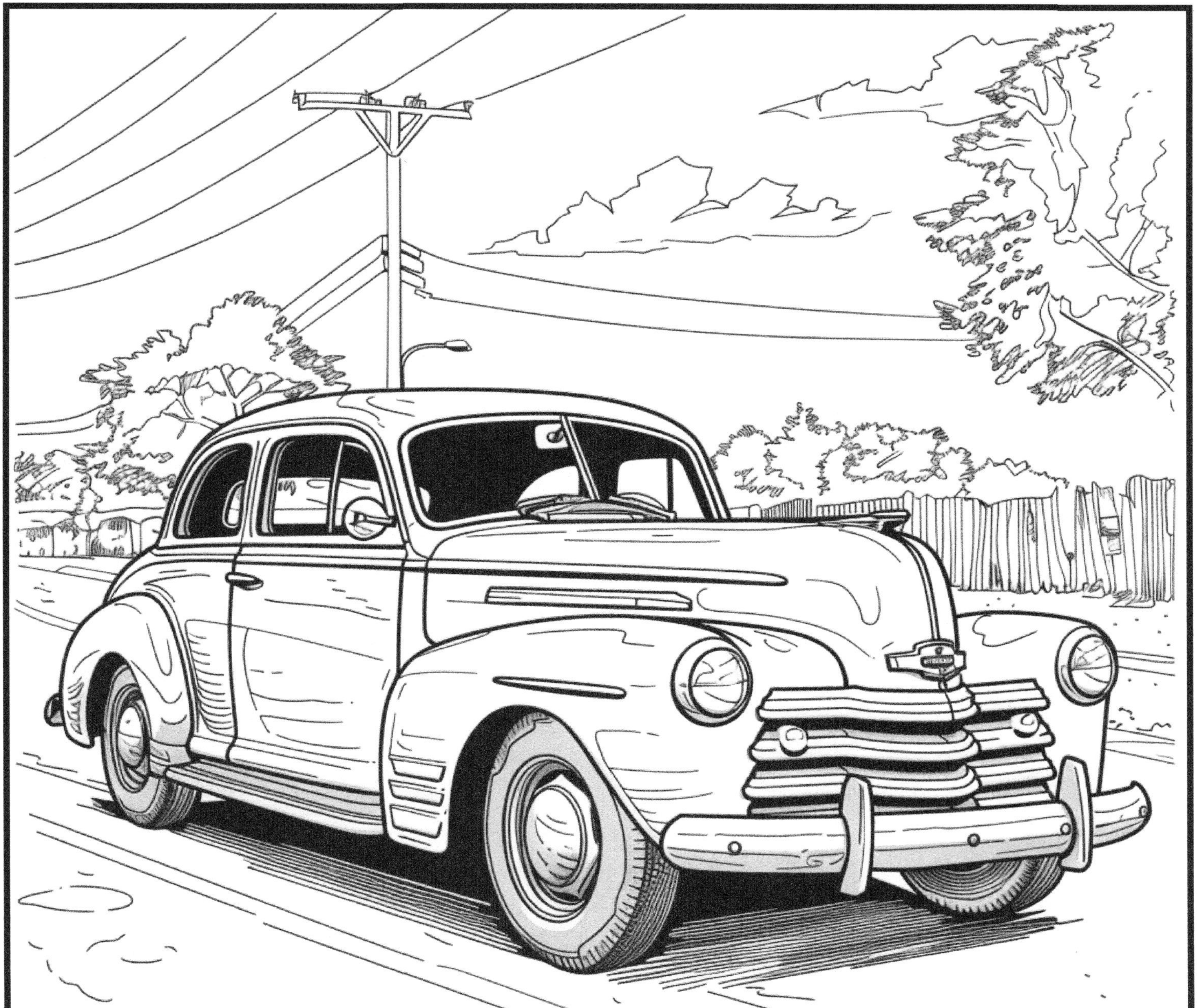

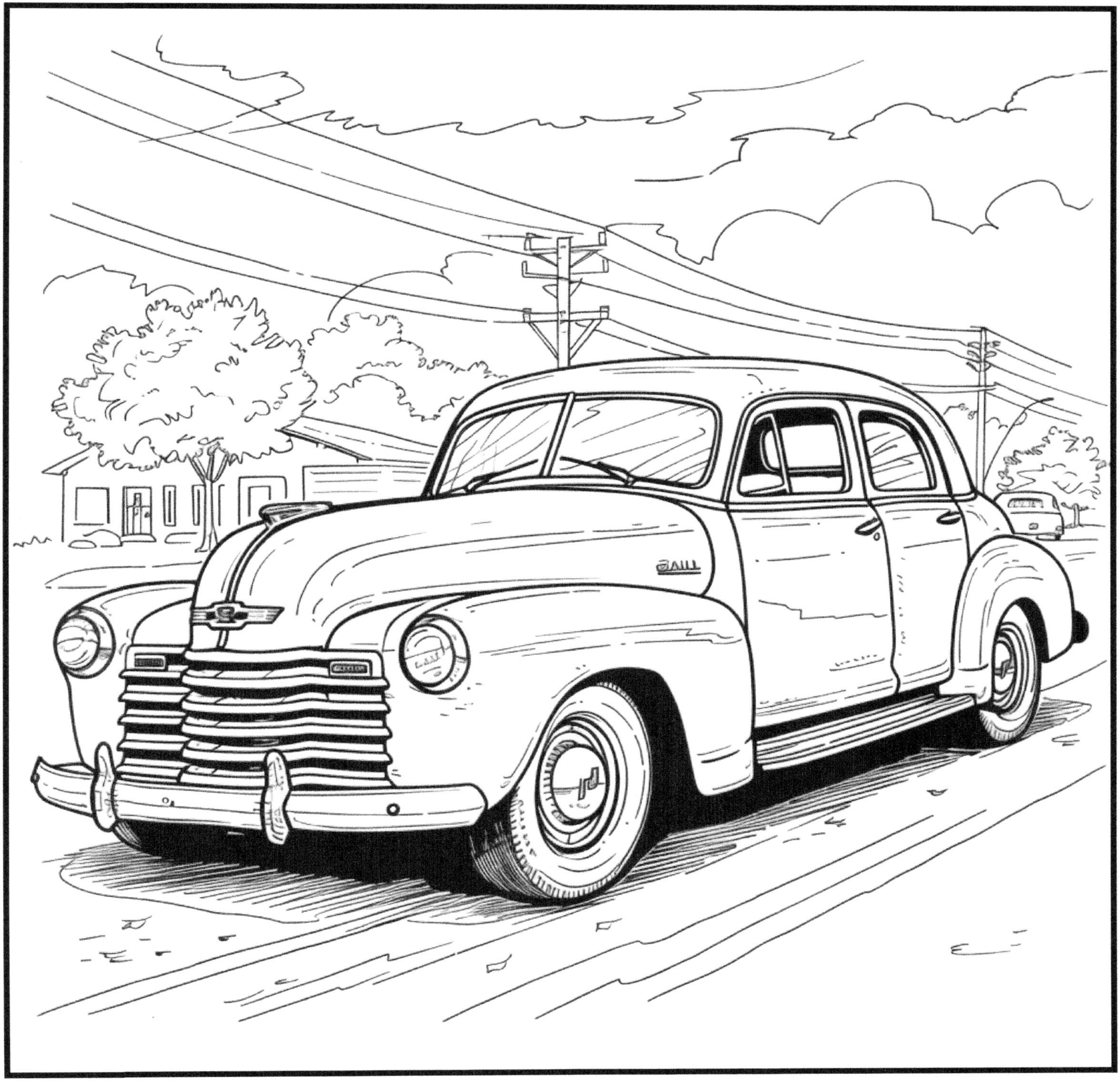

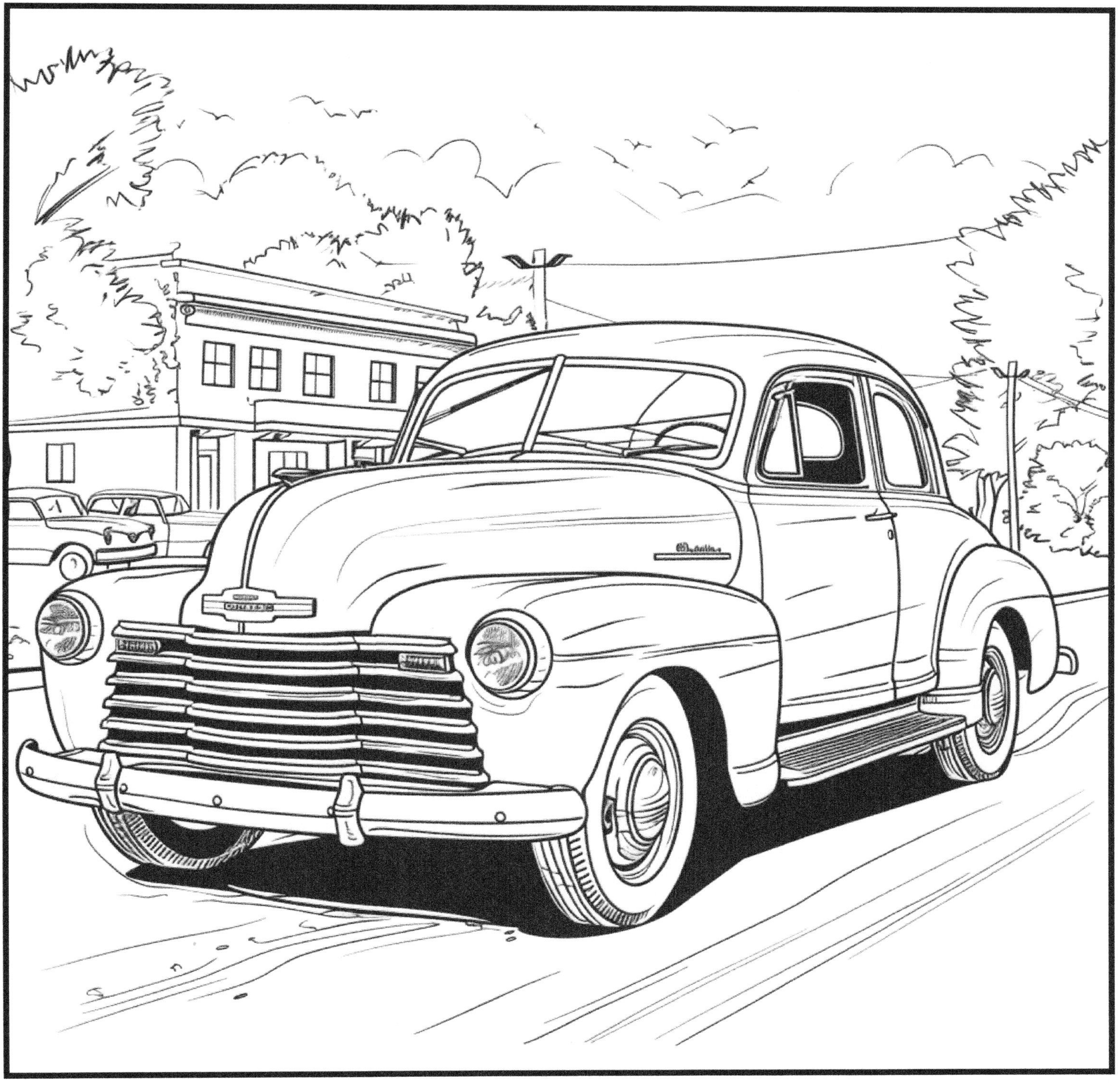

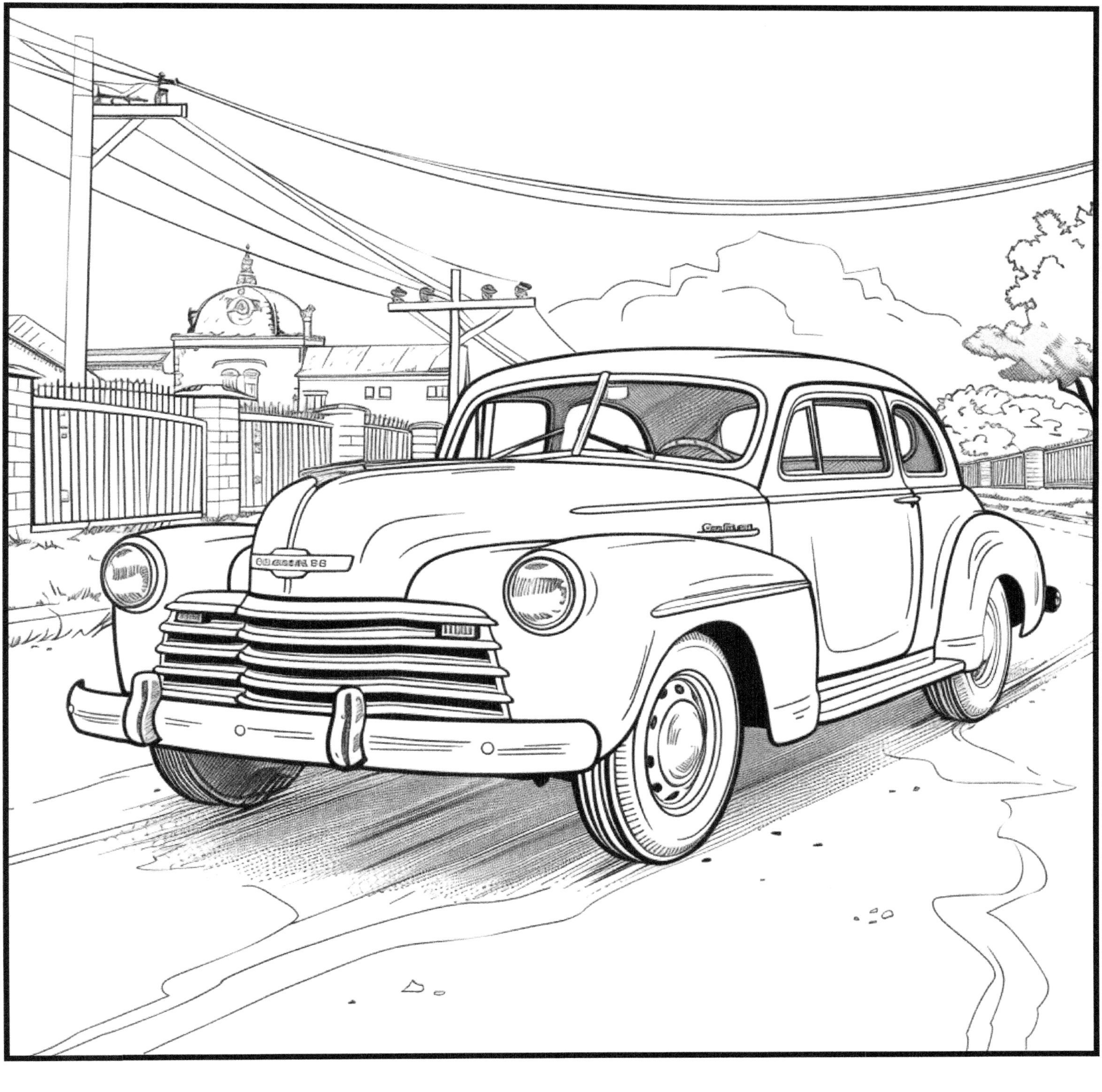

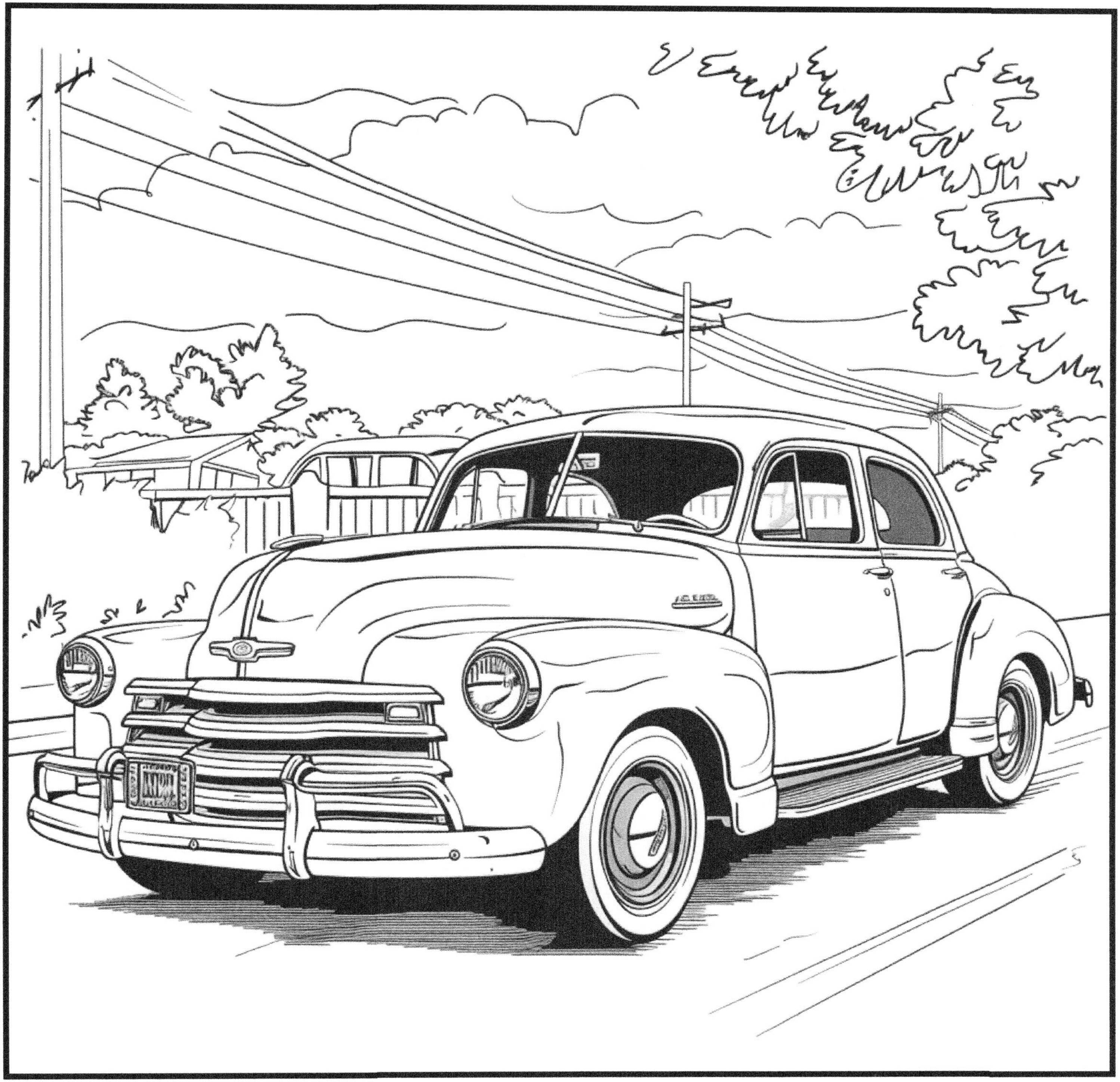

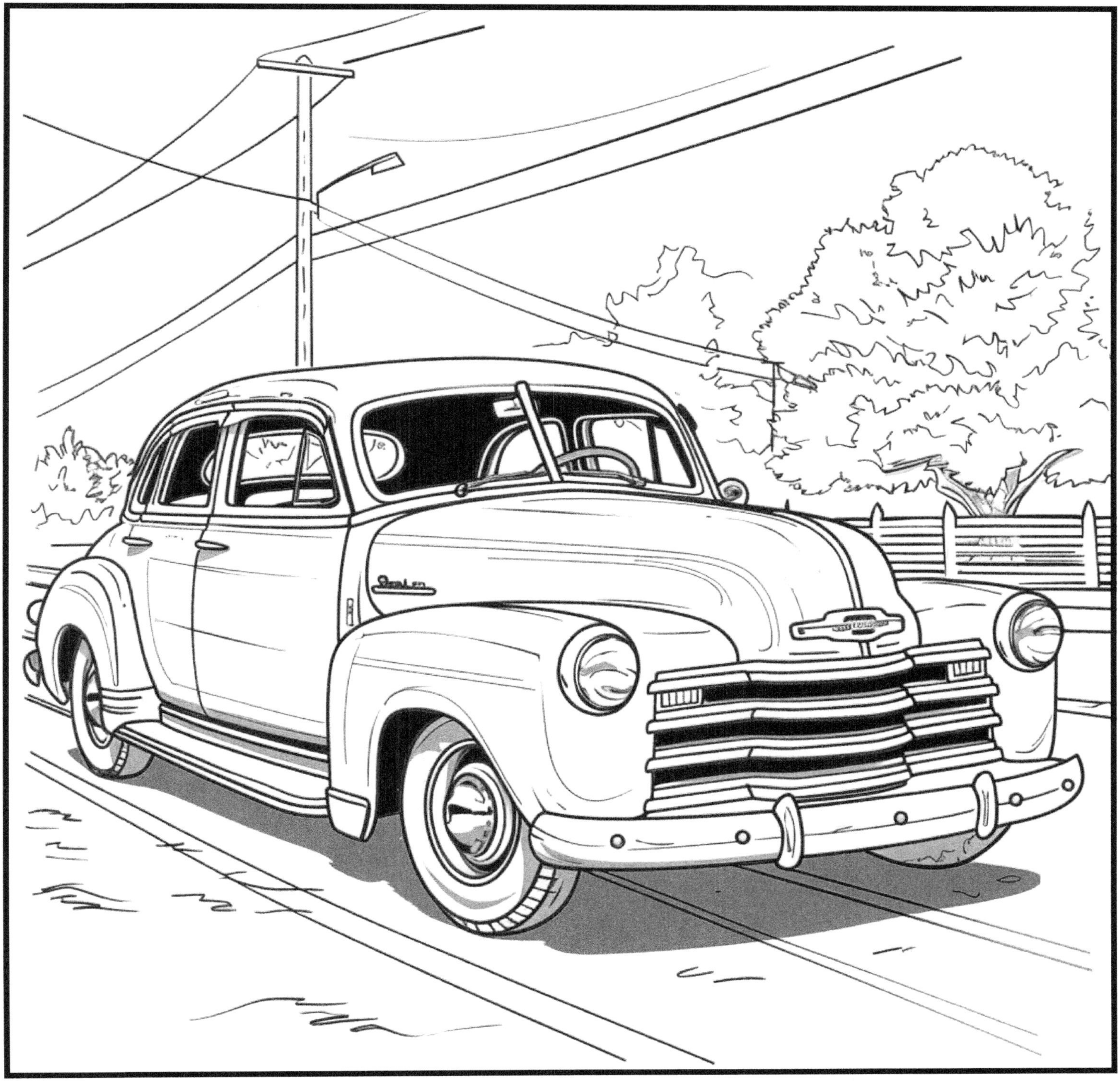

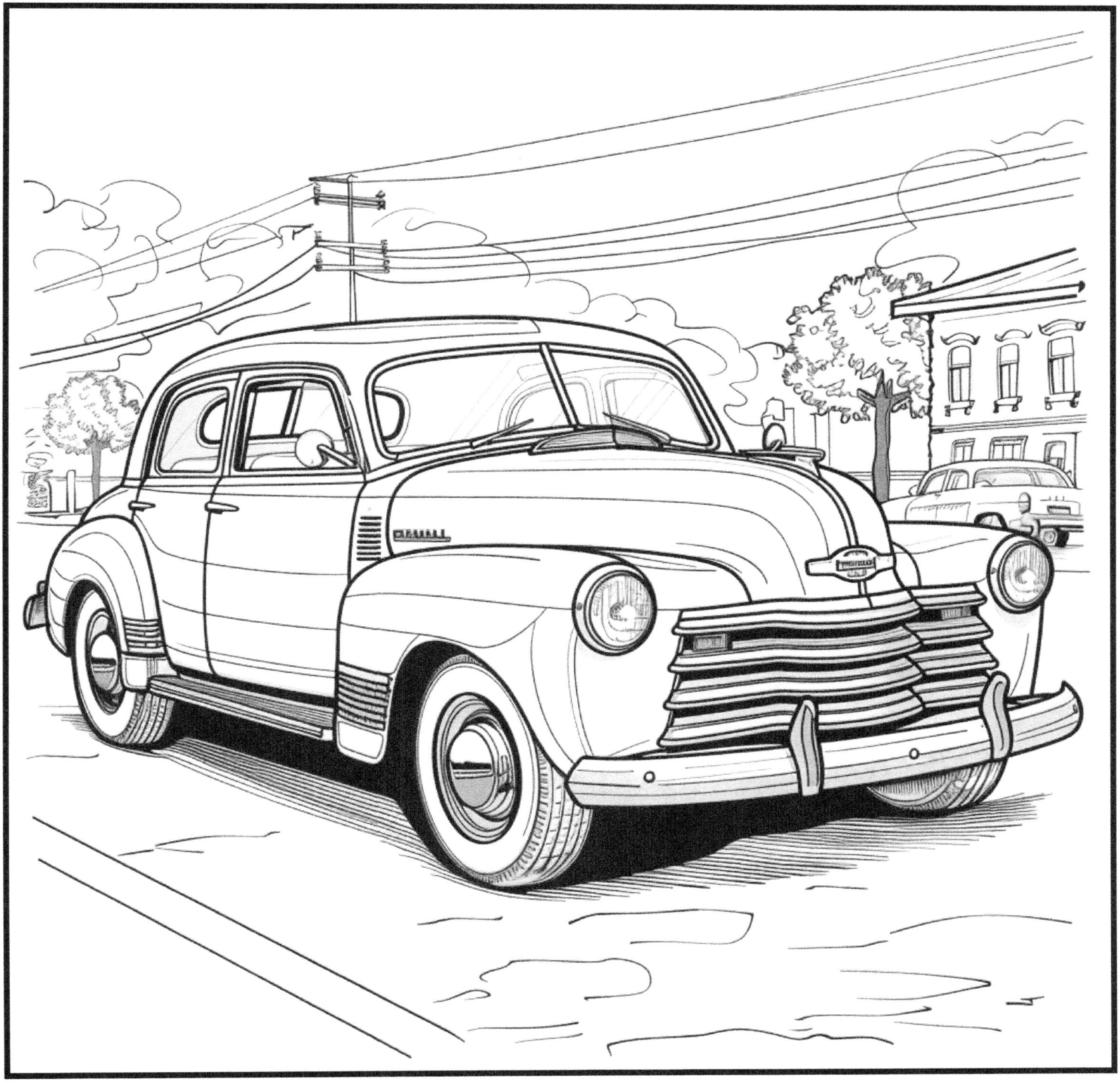

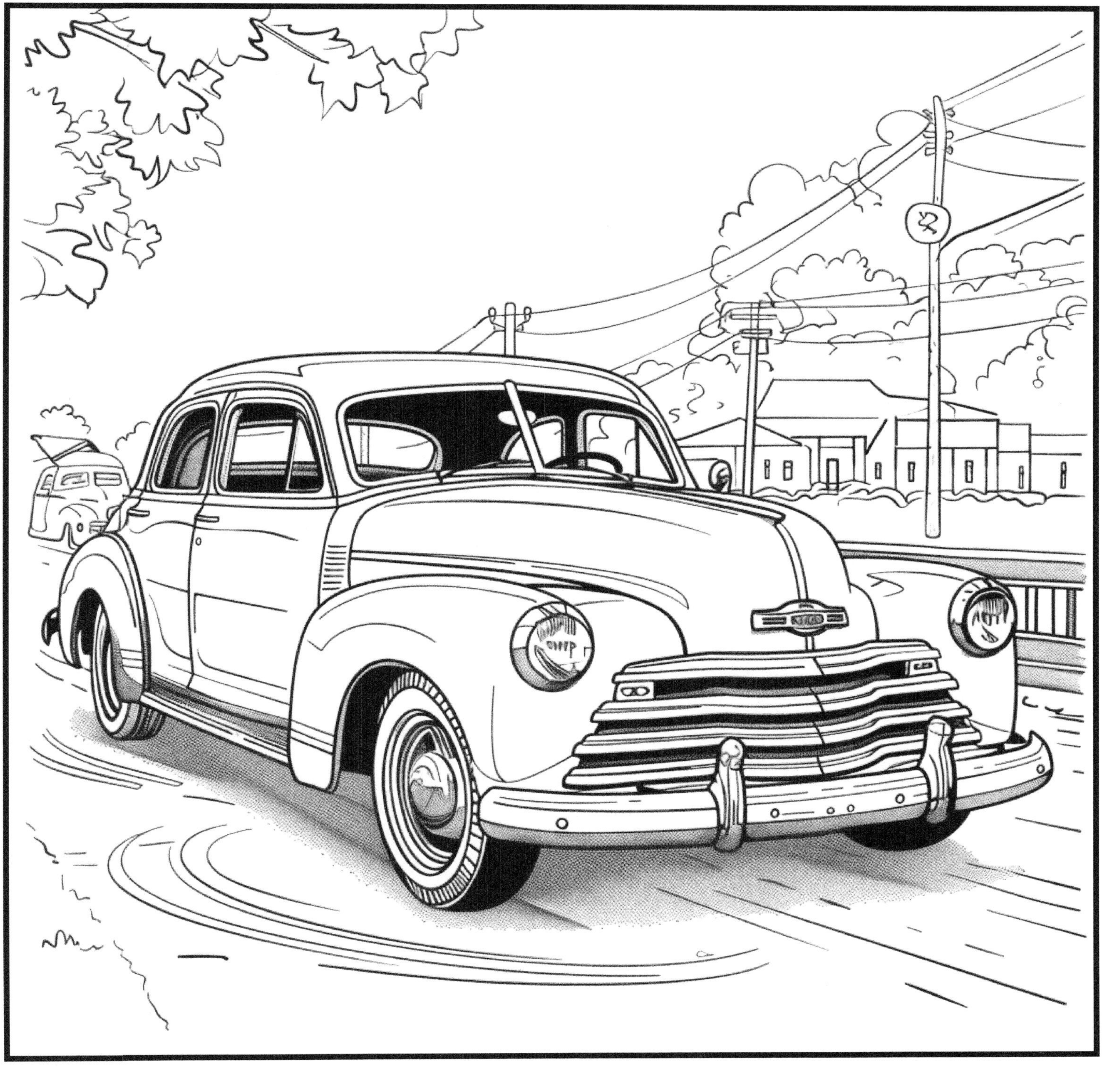

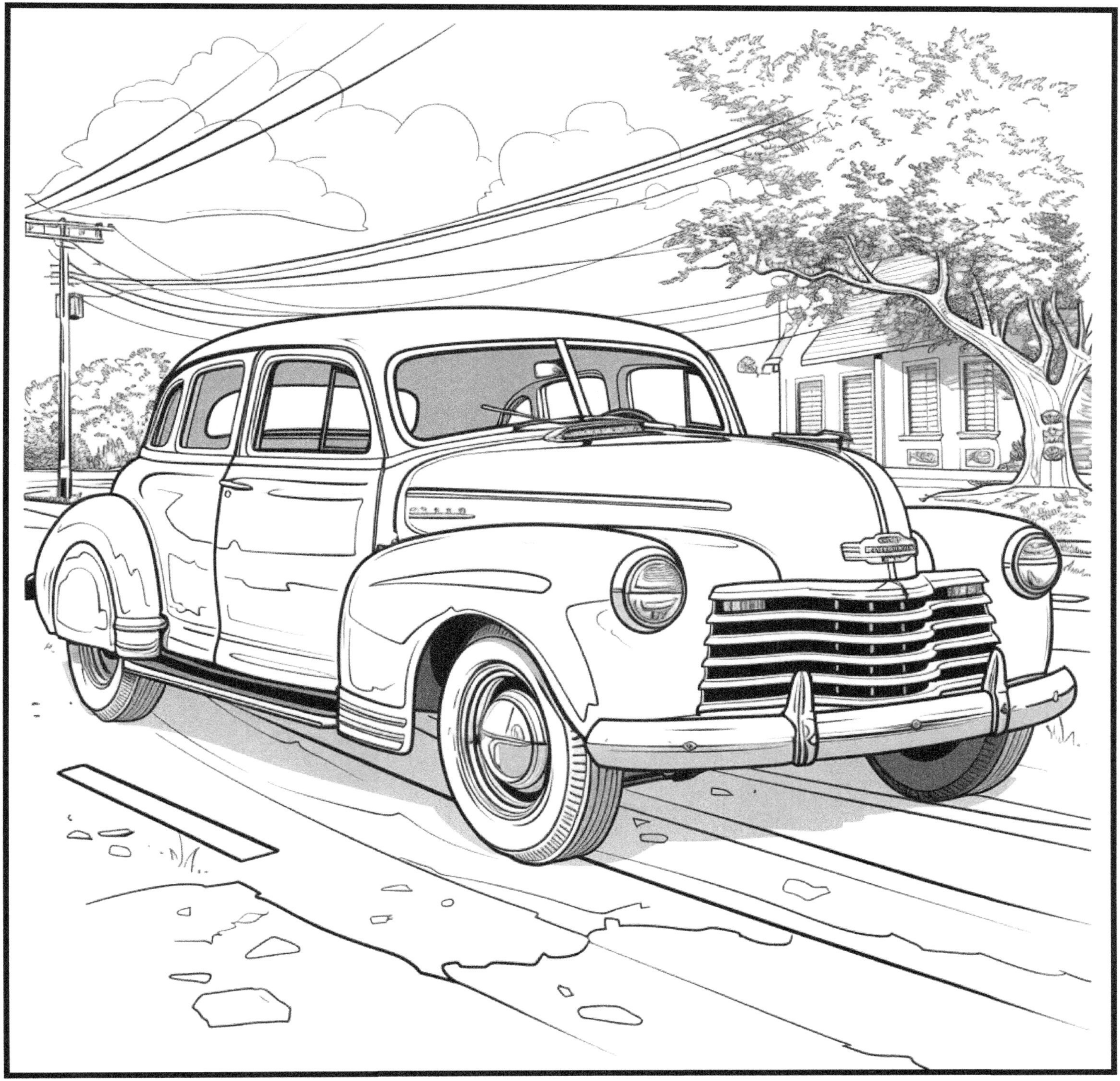

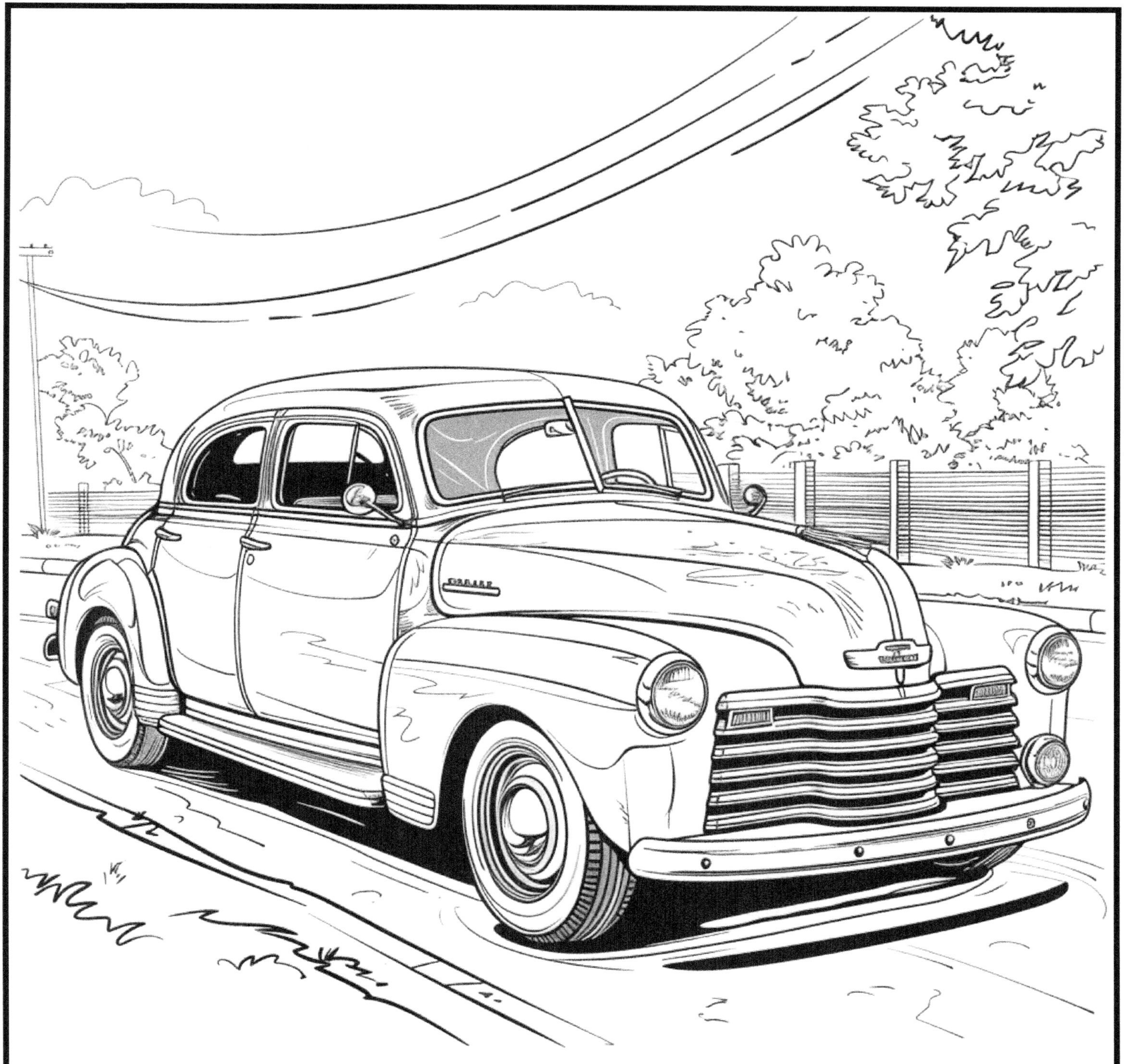

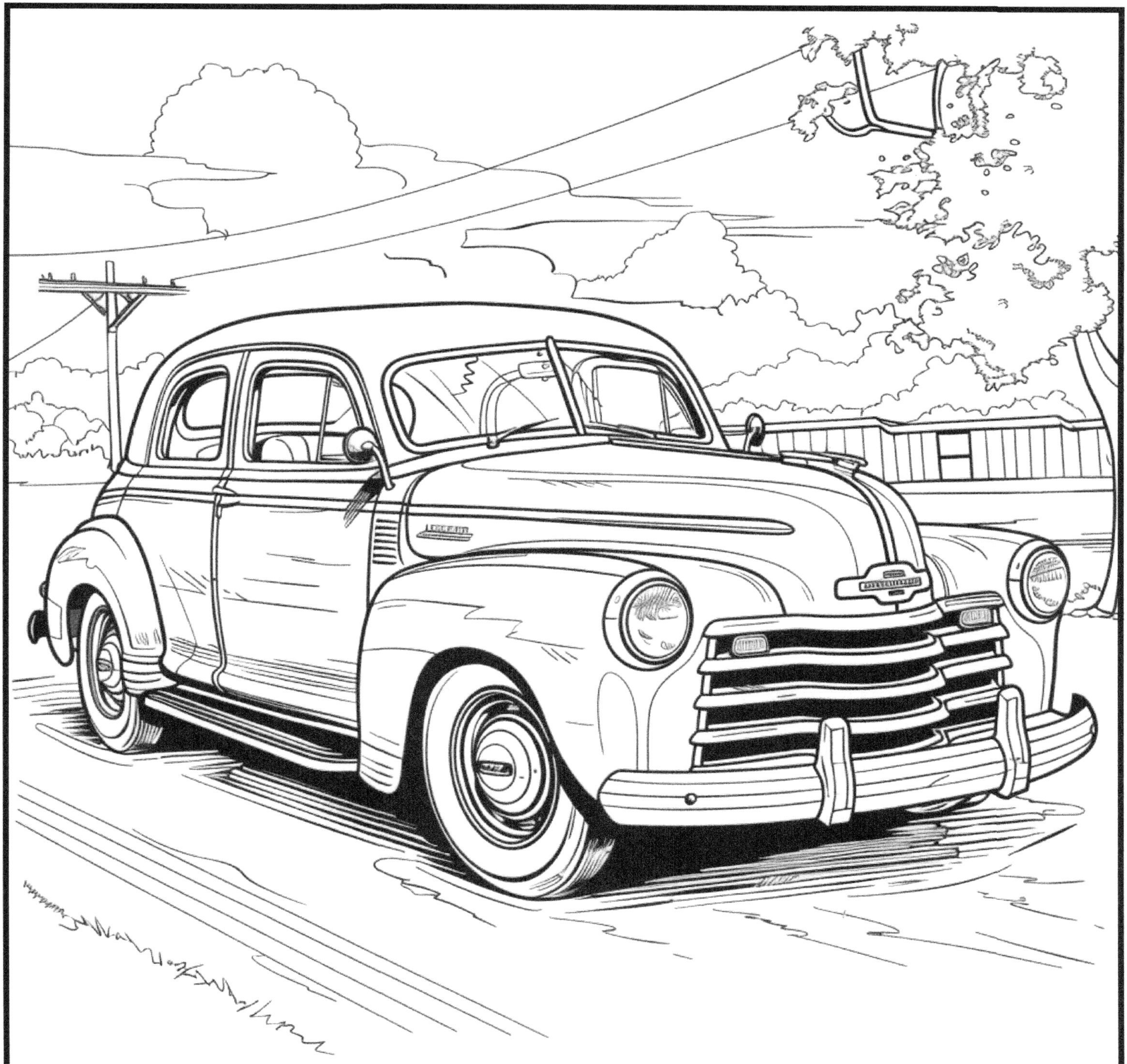

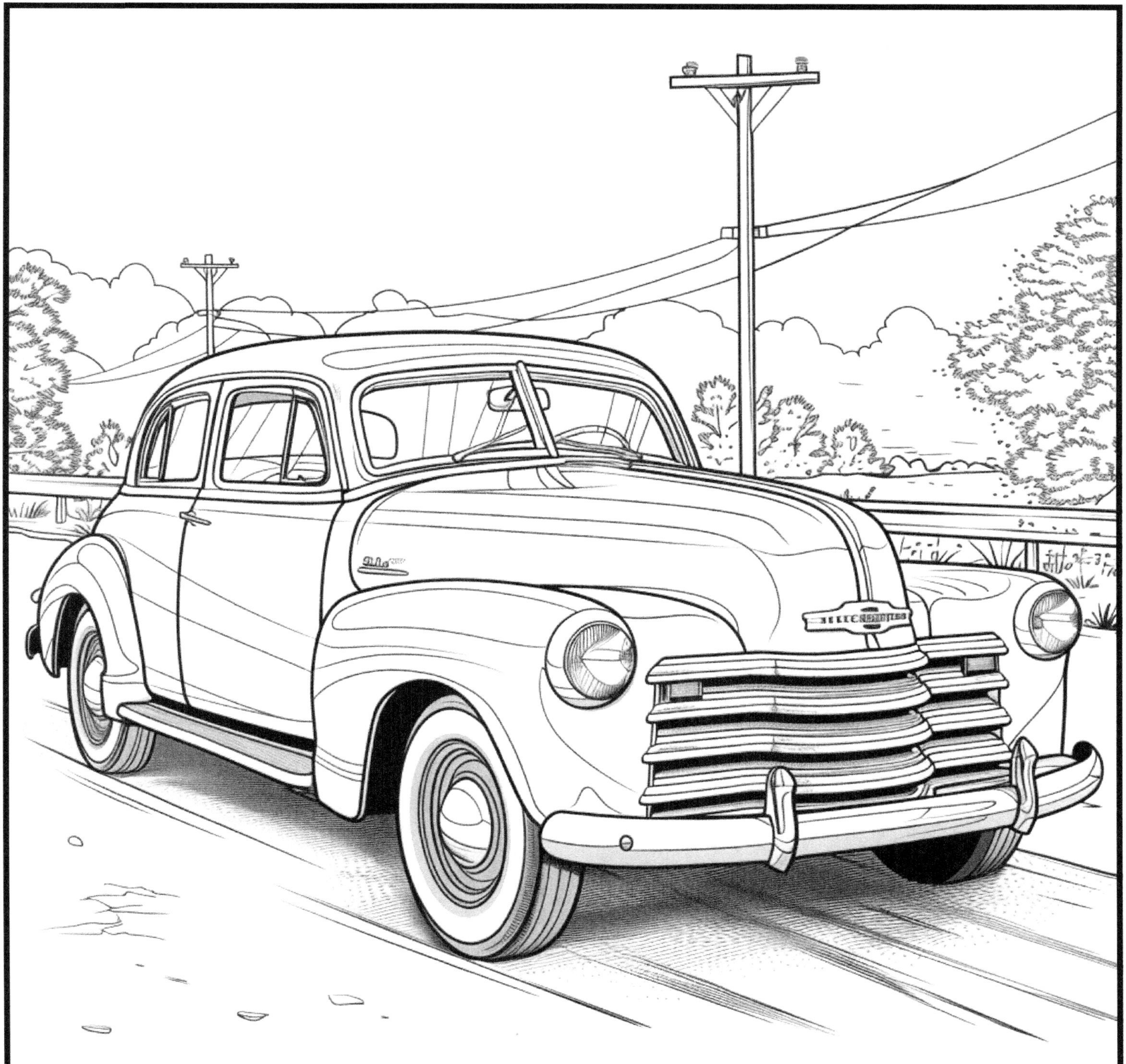

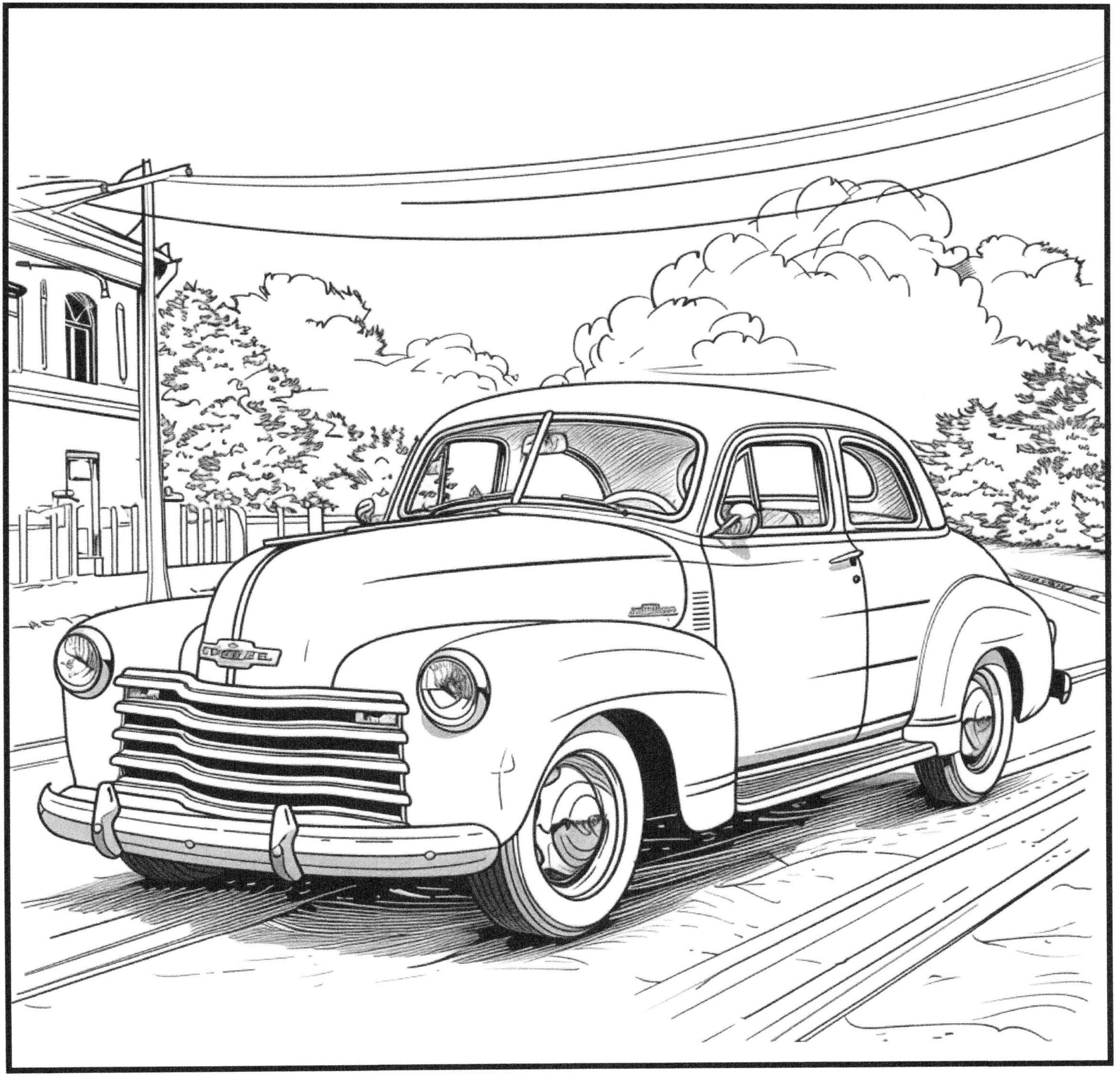

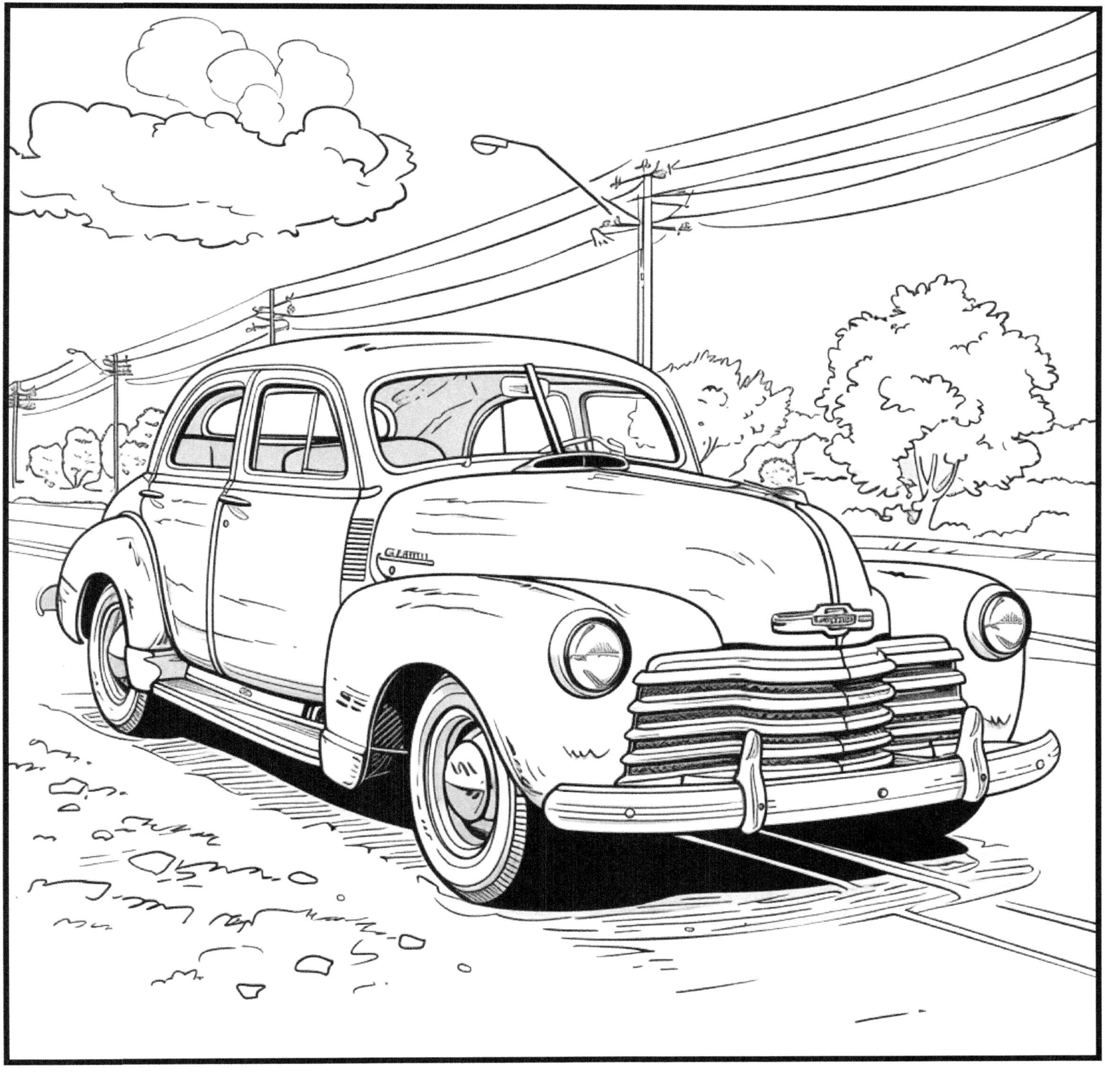

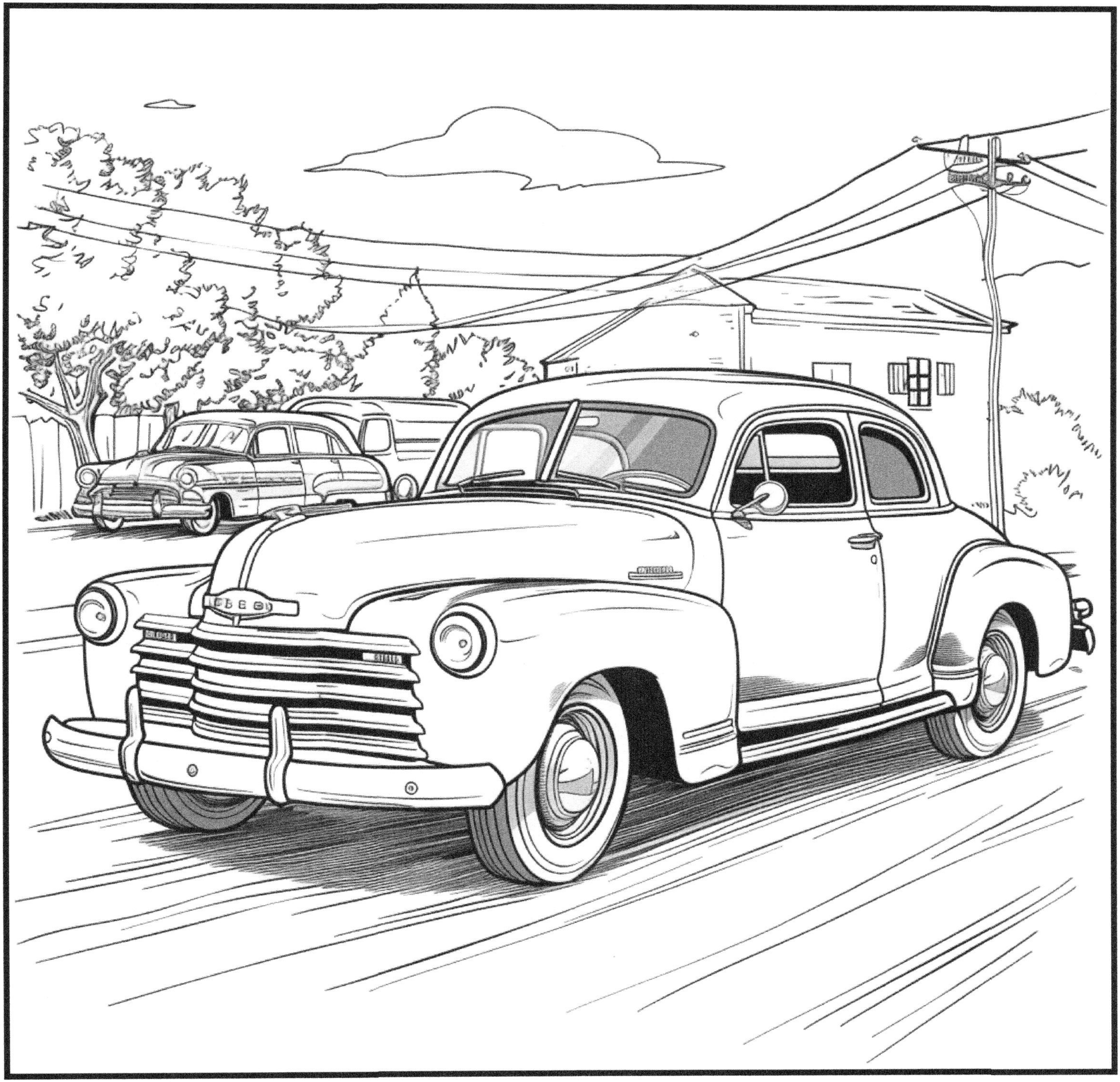

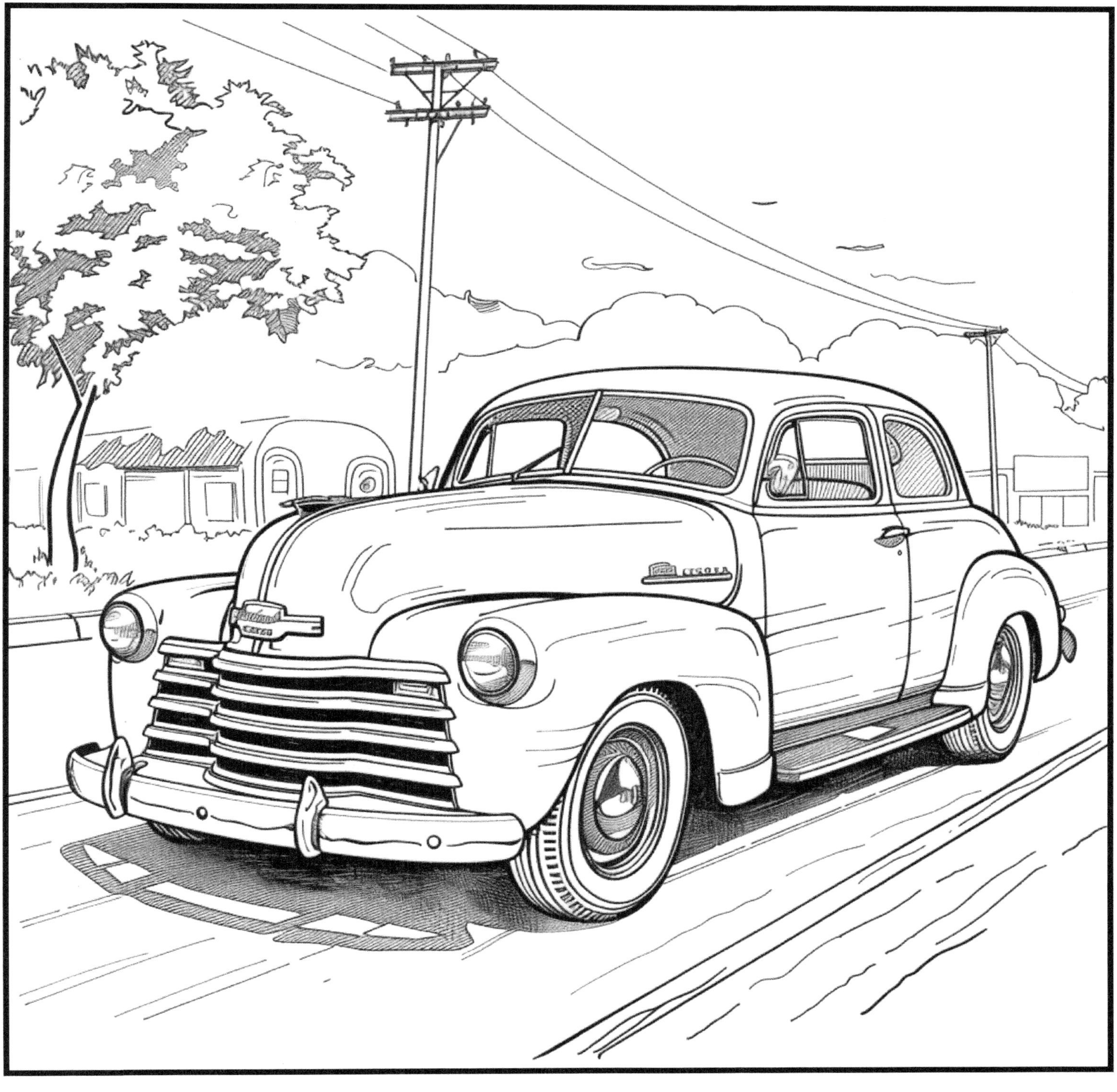

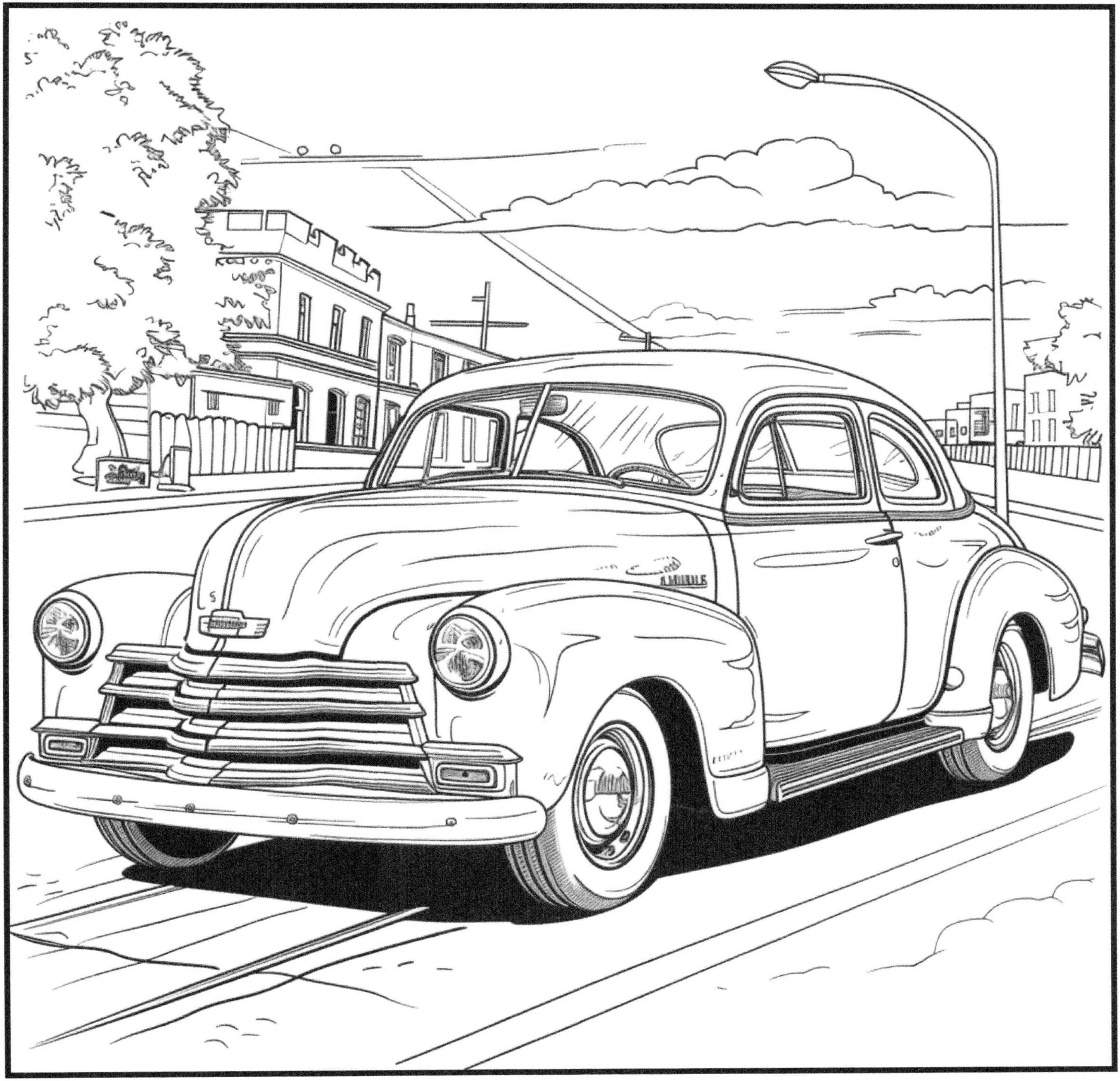

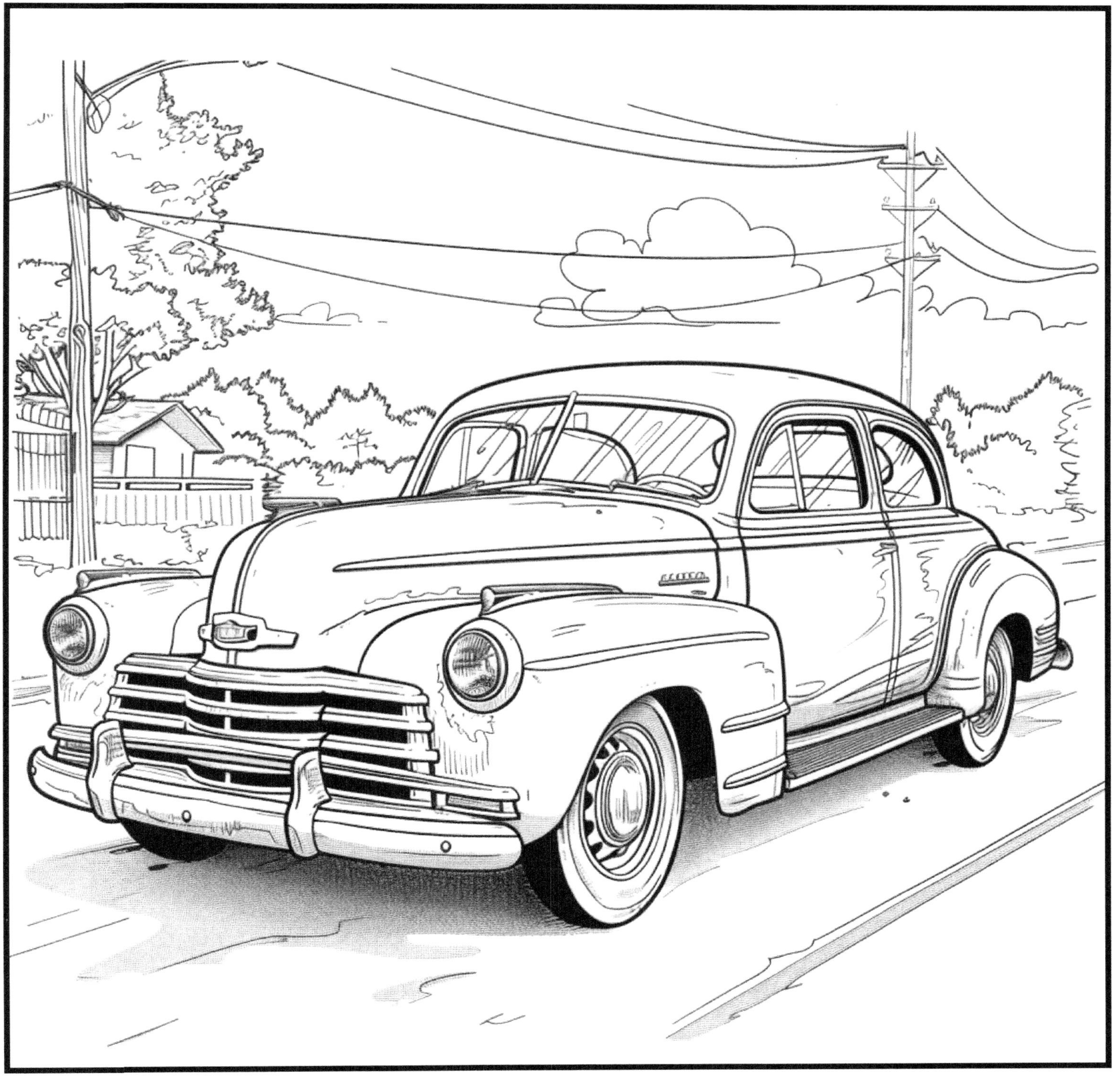

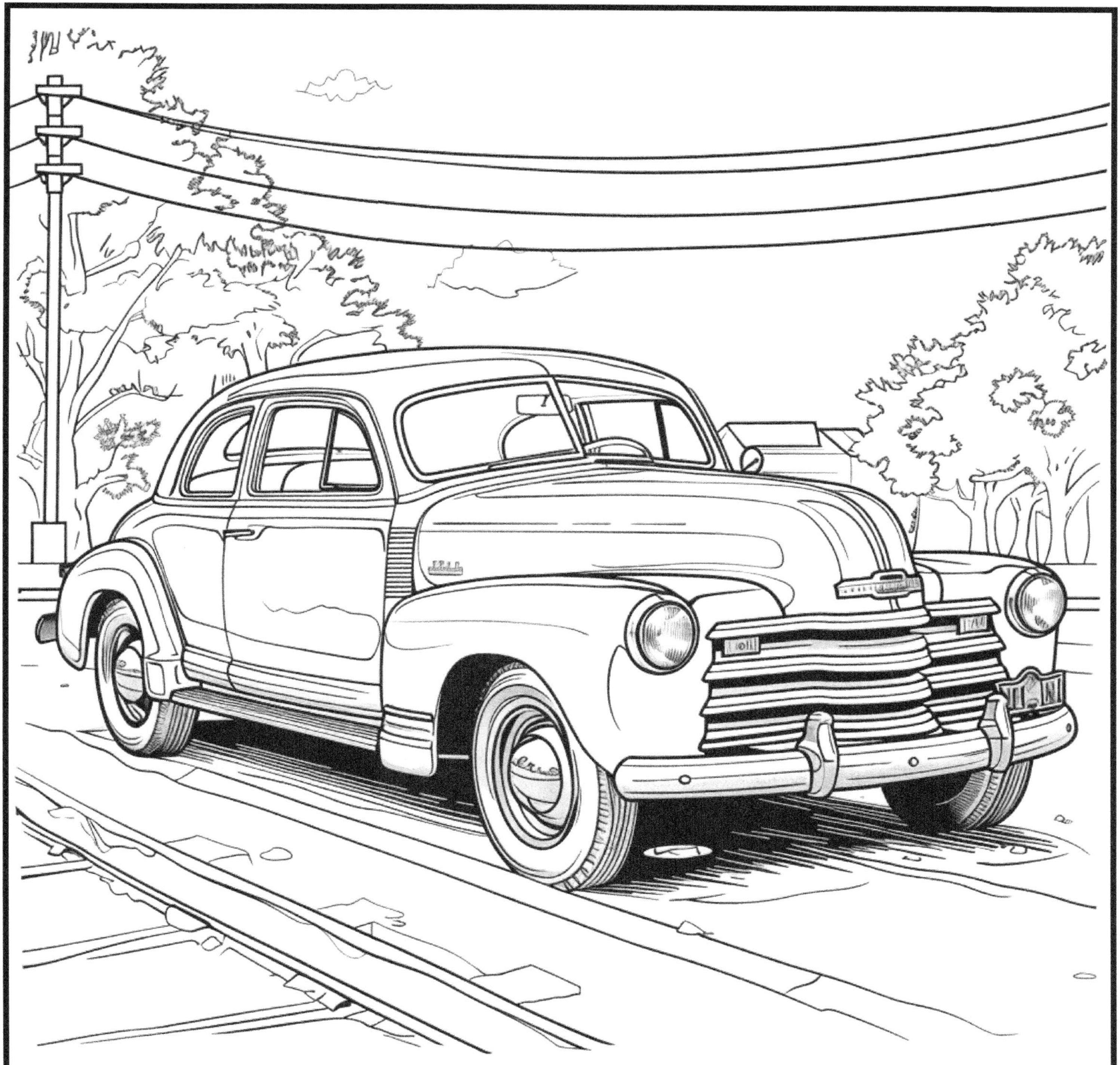

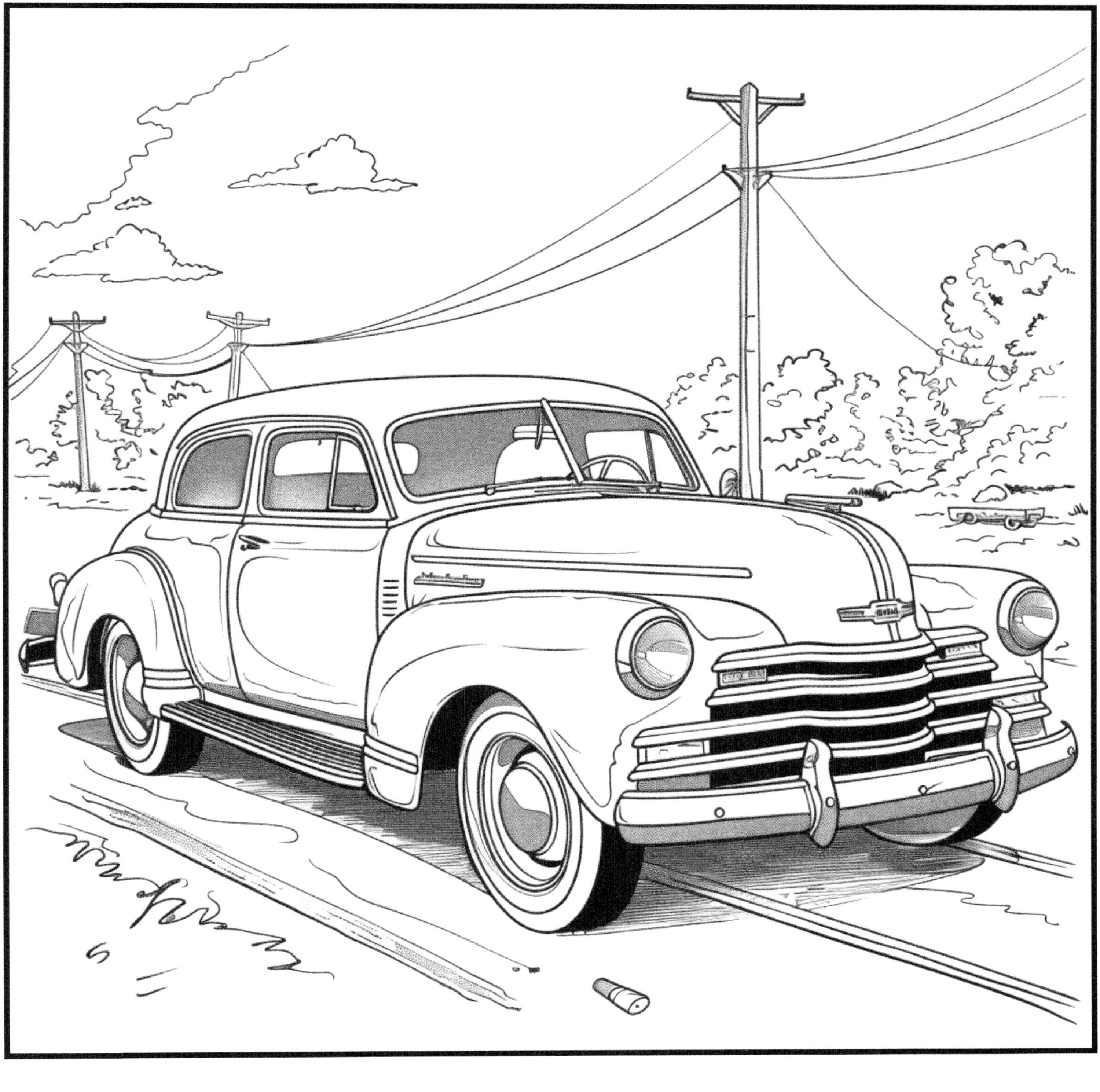

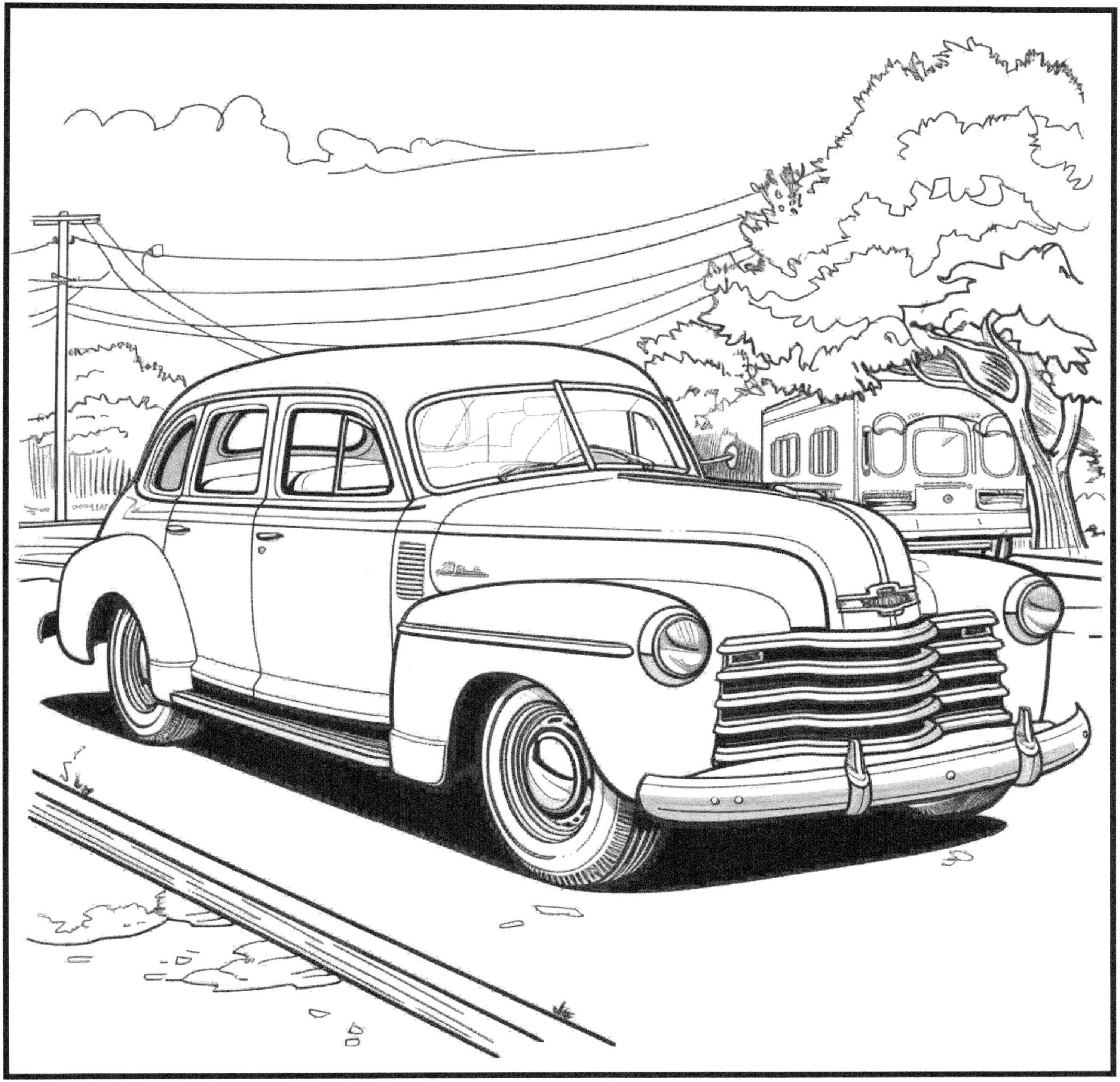

Printed in Great Britain
by Amazon

54799810R00046